THE **PROFIT**
PROBLEM

THE PROFIT PROBLEM

They Say
I MAKE MONEY
So Why
DON'T I HAVE ANY?

MARTIN T. HOLLAND

ANNEAL PUBLISHING

Anneal Publishing
Norman, OK

www.annealbc.com

ISBN: 978-1-7346036-2-0 (hardcover)
         978-1-7346036-0-6 (paperback)
         978-1-7346036-1-3 (ebook)

The Lion of St. Mark

The Lion of St. Mark has been the symbol of the City of Venice, Italy and its predecessor, the Maritime Republic of Venice, since the twelfth century. Although they did not invent the system, Venetian merchants adopted and popularized double-entry bookkeeping, which became known as bookkeeping "alla Veneziana," or bookkeeping "Venetian style." Over the centuries, double-entry bookkeeping has become the worldwide standard for recording financial transactions, which places Venice and its bookkeeping style at the tipping point in the evolution of modern commerce, economies, and societies.

A Promise to Pay

We toasted the sale as our most profitable to date.
It was packaged and shipped; we even prepaid the freight.
We burned through our cash to reach that day,
But we weren't worried because they promised to pay.

We imagined ourselves smoking fat cigars
And paying off debt and buying new cars,
But our dreams had to wait for another day,
Because we couldn't spend a promise to pay.

At first, they were polite when accepting our call,
Then reserved, then guarded, then…nothing at all.
Phone or stop by or try what we may,
We couldn't get through to remind them to pay.

Weeks had gone by, then a month, then two,
When our bank began slowly to tighten the screw.
We assured them the funds would arrive any day,
For *surely* they'd make good on their promise to pay.

By the end we had scrambled and done what we could,
But it wasn't enough to do much good.
When they came for our dreams and took them away,
It didn't seem fair. We had promised to pay.

CONTENTS

Section IV Other Benefits of Good Books

INTRODUCTION

Business is not an art or a science. It's a competitive undertaking with rules, winners, losers, ways of keeping scores, and all the elements of luck and talent.

—Jack Stack, *The Great Game of Business*

"They say I make money, so why don't I have any?"

I work with small business owners every day, and I hear that question at least once a week, even more often around tax time. That's when CPAs tell clients how much money they made and deliver their verdicts on taxes due. I'll bet you've asked the question yourself, "If I made so damn much money, where is it?" Answer that question and you will change your life.

It is impossible to keep track of cash entirely in our heads. I know, because I've tried it myself, and I've seen hundreds of business owners try it without success. Bank statements and apps don't work either, as you've surely discovered, and we will see why in the following pages.

There are ample rewards for owning and managing a business, including autonomy, purpose, respect, and a sense of accomplishment. Unfortunately, those rewards are routinely offset by stress, lost family time, financial difficulties, indecision, and fear. Much of the suffering is due to the lack of good information. It doesn't have to be that way. Jim Rohn, the great business philosopher, said, "If the prize is apparent, the price is easy." The prizes for understanding bookkeeping information are less stress, more free time, better decisions, and more money. The price? The price is minimal because you don't have to become a bookkeeper or accountant to benefit. In fact, you shouldn't. You have only to recognize good books, to insist on them in your business, and to make good use of the information they provide.

In addition to worrying about cash, have you ever asked any of the following questions?

- Am I making money?

- Can I afford to hire more people?

- What will happen if I change my prices?

- How can I double my profit without doubling my effort?

- How much money do I need to grow?

- Why are sales up but profits are down?

- Is there a better way to make decisions other than following my "gut?"

- What should I do about competitors' discounts?

- What is my business worth, and what can I do about it?

- What is breakeven, and why should I care about it?

- What's all that stuff my bank wants?

- How do I set targets for my sales team?

- How is it that I used to know everything but now I'm lost?

- Why are all the business owners around me doing so well while I'm suffering?

Regarding the last question, take heart. I often hear it from small business owners. I assure you that beneath their apparent calm, other business owners are struggling with the same issues and wondering the same things—and, as we will see, it has been that way for centuries.

Begin by accepting that you need financial information to make decisions and money in business. Numbers are the language of business, and you cannot thrive as a financial illiterate. You can't even do a decent job. You must know what the score is, how it's kept, and what to do about it.

I love this stuff. I understand that you may not, but I hope you come to appreciate and benefit from bookkeeping and the ingenious solutions worked out over the centuries by countless others who came before you and wrestled with the same issues you now face.

I have been active in small business since 1974. Prior to becoming a business coach in 2011, I helped start or reorganize six small businesses in industries ranging from biotechnology, contracting and chemical sales to agricultural commodities and manufacturing. Two of the businesses failed. I (and my partners) sold the other four. I began business with absolutely no training in bookkeeping or any idea that it could be useful for anything more than paying taxes. I quickly learned otherwise as I embarrassed myself trying to bluff my way through meetings with bankers, investors, and seasoned businesspeople as I attempted to raise millions of dollars. I was a financial illiterate and it showed. I discovered that it was impossible to raise money, to make good operating decisions, to plan, or to value and sell a company without objective information. As you will see throughout this book, I also learned that ignorance when it comes to bookkeeping and financial reports can ruin lives.

The difficult news is that we will have to discuss a few numbers, which may require some concentration on your part. The good news is that we will keep the numbers to a minimum, and it will be well worth the effort. You'll also be happy to know that *you* won't have to record the numbers or compile the reports, nor will you ever have to use debits and credits if you choose not to. We will discuss them because they are at the foundation of the fascinating history of business but you won't have to use them. All of that is the job of your bookkeeper or accountant. Your role will be to understand the reports bookkeeping makes possible and to know how to use them to make better decisions and more money. Peter Drucker, who has been described as the founder of modern business management, is credited with saying, "What gets measured, gets managed." My experience has shown that what gets *managed* gets better. Numbers are at the foundation of management.

In the pages that follow, I'll address the list of questions above and more—or rather, I will give you the practical information and tools you need to address them for *your* business using *your* financial statements. *What?* You don't have financial statements? Well, you'll want to fix that after reading this book. You should read this book first so you have both the ability to recognize proper financial statements and a burning desire to acquire them. If you already receive regular financial statements, that's a significant head start on most of your small business peers but, as you will see, the statements may need to be rearranged a little to become *really* useful.

This book is arranged in four sections that follow the process I use to teach my coaching clients about bookkeeping and financial reports. Section I provides context by answering *why* bookkeeping is so important. It begins with an overview of the deep, rich history of bookkeeping, explains why our ancestors developed it in the first place, and why it is as important today as it was centuries ago. The section explains the objective purpose of business, demonstrates how subconscious attitudes about money deeply affect results, and delivers eight rational arguments in defense of profit. You will learn to recognize good books and understand why profits not only *are* good but also *do* good.

Section II strips all numbers and math from the three standard financial reports to examine their purpose and form. You will see why the reports were created and what they can tell you about your business.

Section III puts some numbers back into the reports and shows you by example how to use numbers to make better decisions and more money.

Section IV is a look at important issues that affect or are affected by bookkeeping and financial reports.

All the stories in this book are based on real people, companies, and events. I have changed the names and some other details in order to protect my innocence.

My father told me a story about the poet Robert Frost and his friend, who were walking down a sidewalk after a party in New York City. His friend walked into a tree that knocked her over backward. As Frost knelt beside her, he asked:

"Didn't you see the tree?"

"Yes, Robert, I saw it," she answered, "*but I didn't realize it.*"

You may have seen or heard of many of the things that follow. I hope this book prompts you to have realizations.

SECTION I

YOU ARE NOT ALONE

CHAPTER 1

The Origins of Bookkeeping

Take things always by the smooth handle.

—Thomas Jefferson

M OST OF US IN BUSINESS UNDERSTAND THE NEED TO KEEP TRACK OF our financial transactions. If for no other reason, we understand that we need the information to pay taxes and avoid trouble. Beyond that, most of us have a visceral need to know where we stand financially. We are lost or at least anxious when we don't.

Tracking financial transactions is known as "bookkeeping" because transactions that are now recorded as computer files were until very recently recorded in actual books. A special type of bookkeeping—the type that works best, enables commerce, and plays a prominent role in this book—is called "double-entry bookkeeping." We'll see soon why it's called double-entry.

Even those familiar with double-entry bookkeeping are unlikely to know of its foundation, laid by a Venetian monk named Luca Pacioli.[1] In his book, *Details of Computation and Recording*, Pacioli was the first to write out the rules of double-entry bookkeeping. At the time his book was first lifted from

---

1 It takes a sophisticated guy to compile a sophisticated system, and Luca Pacioli certainly fit the bill. It is widely accepted that he taught Leonardo da Vinci the linear perspective for which his painting of *The Last Supper* is famous.

a Gutenberg press in 1494 AD, the rules of bookkeeping had been around for about 200 years. They have survived unchanged and are in universal use today—or would be if we all kept up our end of the bargain.

It is reasonable to ask why these rules have endured so long, but any twenty-first century business owner will recognize the three things Pacioli says are essential to business:

1. "Cash, or any equivalent. Without this, business can hardly be carried on."

2. "Rules" for recording transaction "so that the diligent reader can understand [what happened] all by himself."

3. "A systematic way to understand transactions *at a glance*."

Without these things, Pacioli says, "It would be impossible for merchants to conduct their business, for they would have no rest and their minds would always be troubled." Does any of that sound familiar?

What fifteenth century issues could possibly trouble the minds of a modern-day business owner? In addition to cash and understanding individual transactions, any business owner—past, present, or future—would be troubled without answers to these five questions:

1. Am I making money?

2. What do I own?

3. What do I owe?

4. What's left over for me?

5. Where did my cash go?

Dive into those questions and you will find that they lead to even more questions about sales, expenses, inventory, receivables, payables, long-term debt, property, taxes, dividends, audit, embezzlement, and so on. Uncertainty surrounding these issues troubled merchants centuries ago and troubles business owners today.

Double-entry bookkeeping has not changed because the issues it resolves have not changed. I mention this history not only because I love it and find it fascinating but also so that you may find comfort in the knowledge that your issues are timeless and common. You are not alone.

CHAPTER 2

The Triple-Double of Double-Entry Bookkeeping

I do not wish to break my brain trying to comprehend something which I do not understand now, nor have I understood in all my days.

—Philip II, King of Spain, 1574,
from *The Reckoning* by Jacob Soll

W HEN I FIRST ENCOUNTERED DOUBLE-ENTRY BOOKKEEPING, I PRE-
sumed it was named that because, as we will see shortly, every entry must be recorded twice—once as a debit and once as a credit. Although debits and credits probably account for the name, I soon discovered that there are two more doubles required by good bookkeeping practices. Together, they make up the triple-double of double-entry bookkeeping, which is:

1. Every transaction must be recorded as both a debit and a credit.

2. Every transaction must be recorded in both a journal and a ledger.

3. Every transaction must be recorded in the books of both parties.

If that sounds like a lot of doubles, it is. However, *you must at least be aware* of all three in order to fully understand your business and the benefits of bookkeeping, as you will see below.

It's reasonable to ask how Pacioli's antique rules could possibly address all the issues faced by a modern business. The answer is in the name "double-entry." The rules of double-entry require every transaction to be recorded twice, once as a debit and once as a credit. To understand the process, think of one entry (the debit) as recording "where it went," the other (the credit) as recording "where it came from." Let's see how it works and why it matters.

Consider a simple transaction such as a plumber selling an hour of his services for $200. Double-entry requires him to record both where the money went (to his bank account) and where it came from (sales). Now suppose the plumber *borrowed* $1,000. He would record where the money went (again, to his bank account) and where it came from (this time, a loan). By looking at the paired entries, a diligent reader could understand both transactions all by himself at a glance. The reader could see immediately that one deposit was income and the other a loan.

Contrast that example with the same transactions recorded as "single entries" in a bank register. This time, the plumber simply records both his sale and his loan as deposits in his bank account totaling $1,200. That's it. He knows that $1,200 went into the bank because he recorded the entries in his bank register, but he has no idea where the money came from unless he remembers, which should be easy for two recent transactions. However, it would be impossible to recall hundreds or thousands of transactions over time, and the resulting uncertainty would lead to a troubled mind and the unrest that makes it impossible to conduct business. If you've been in business for any length of time, you know exactly what I mean, don't you?

To see an example of why complete information matters, assume that income is taxable, loans are not, and that our diligent reader is an IRS agent. "Well, now," says the agent. "I see $1,200 dollars in deposits on your bank statement. That's income. Give me my taxes."

The plumber protests that $1,000 was a loan and not taxable, to which the agent replies, "Prove it." The plumber may be able to do so by gathering documents from scattered sources, but neither he nor the agent could do so at a glance.

We can see the problem clearly in the example of a used furniture dealer. This dealer was in the business of buying junk for cash at garage sales on weekends. He would clean up his purchases and resell them as rare treasures. "We buy junk, we sell antiques." To fund his buying expeditions, he routinely withdrew cash from his bank on Fridays and redeposited any unspent cash the following week—lots of $1,000 or $2,000 withdrawals one week, followed by lots of random deposits the next week. We can imagine what his bank statement looked like. His deposits were made up of new money from sales along with unspent money from the prior week's withdrawals. It was virtually impossible to distinguish between the two by looking at his bank statements or to tell how many times the same money had been withdrawn and redeposited. It was impossible to understand any of the transactions at a glance.

Like many of us, the dealer didn't keep books, so when the IRS showed up to audit him, they had only his bank statements to review. The auditor simply added up the deposits and called it income. What a mess. If it were you, how would you sort it out? Scramble around looking for sales tickets that don't exist? Implore the IRS agent for mercy? Assure the agent that you remember this or that transaction? None of those tactics is likely to work. In the end, there is little doubt that the IRS overstated the dealer's income. The dealer and the IRS worked out a settlement, but there is also little doubt that he paid more taxes than he would have had he kept good books.

The above examples involved bank deposits, but double-entry rules apply to all transactions, including expenditures. Returning to our plumber, let's suppose he writes two $100 checks and records them in his bank register. One check is for supplies and the other is a repayment of principal on his loan. By looking at his bank register, all he knows is that his balance is now $1,000. He cannot know by simply looking that he has both incurred an expense and reduced his debt. After a year of single-entry transactions, it is safe to say that our plumber would have no idea what his income and expenses were, whether he made a profit, or what he owes on his loan. He is completely lost, and we haven't yet begun to consider the many other types of transactions that trouble the minds of business owners.

We saw above that our furniture dealer's bank statements showed withdrawals as well as deposits. We could argue, as the dealer surely did, that the money from withdrawals was used to buy furniture and pay expenses. If he could prove that, the expenditures would offset at least some of the deposits to reduce both his net profit and his tax bill. Unfortunately, it doesn't work that way. In an audit, taxpayers have to prove expense and a withdrawal by itself doesn't do that. It might have been used to buy furniture for resale or to pay an expense, but it also might have been used to repay debt or to buy the kids parasail rides in the Bahamas. Again, without good books (not to mention receipts), the dealer was defenseless in the audit.

We've now seen that every transaction should be recorded twice, as a debit and a credit. But there is more. The second double of the bookkeeping triple-double is the process of recording every debit and credit in two places. That's right. We must record both sides of each transaction, and we must record both sides in two places. One of the two places (the journal) keeps the entries together, one above the other, so the reader can tell at a glance what happened in the transaction: "This $200 came from income and went to the bank."

PLUMBER'S JOURNAL			
Date	Account	Debit (to)	Credit (from)
Jan 1, 20xx	Bank: First Bank	200.00	
Jan 1, 20xx	Income: plumbing sales		200.00

The second place (a ledger page) accumulates all the entries that affect a single account. That way, the net effect of all the transactions that affect an account, or the account's "balance," can also be seen at a glance. (The plumber's bank register is a ledger page.) This second double is very important because information about both transactions and account balances is essential to business. (After all, our plumber *does* want to know how much he sold, how much he owes, and how much money he has in the bank!) As our plumber discovered, it would be impossible to reconstruct both sides of a transaction from a ledger page alone because only half of the information is there. It would also be overwhelmingly tedious to determine an account balance by searching through transactions in a journal.

PLUMBERS LEDGER PAGE: FIRST BANK				
Date	Account	Debit	Credit	Balance
Jan 1, 20xx	Income: plumbing customer	200.00		200.00
Jan 2, 20xx	Deposit from First Bank loan	1000.00		1,200.00
Jan 3, 20xx	Expense check		100.00	1,100.00
Jan 4, 20xx	First Bank loan repayment		100.00	1,000.00

The first double of the triple-double is the duty to record both sides of every transaction: Where it came from and where it went. The second double is our duty to record every transaction in two places: In a journal and in a ledger. It's now time to look at the third double of the triple-double, one that doesn't require any extra effort on our part if we've kept up with the first two. The third double is the mutual obligation to make equal and opposite entries between separate entities. What the heck does *that* mean? Well, when we make an entry to record a bank deposit in our books (a debit, "where it went"), we rely on the bank to make an equal and opposite entry on our ledger page in *their* books (a credit, "where it came from"). When we reconcile our bank accounts each month, we are simply verifying that we each made the equal and offsetting entries. This responsibility extends beyond the bank. Our customers, our employees, our mortgage companies, our vendors, our partners, our landlords, the IRS—everyone with whom we do business expects us to keep equal and opposite records of our transactions with them.

They expect that they can call us to verify transactions, just like the bank. This is our responsibility to them and theirs to us. The process ties together entire economies because uncertainty, suspicion, and discord would otherwise reign. If we do not keep our end of the bargain, we have shirked our duty and are weak links in the economy. (We are also certain to lose any argument about disputed transactions.)

When we use a bookkeeping program, we may not be aware that we are making journal entries or that the program is posting both sides of the transaction to ledger pages, but we are, and it is. For example, when we write a check in a computer window, we are making a journal entry. Both sides of the transaction are there to be seen at a glance—the "where it came from" account is the bank, and we know that because we are writing a check on our bank account. The "where it went" account is shown clearly on the check stub in the window. The program will not let us click out of the window until we have entered both sides of the transaction. Once entered, most programs allow us to double-click an item to see the current balance for that account on its ledger page.

If you have ever kept books by hand, you understand that one great advantage of a computer program is that it posts journal entries accurately to ledger pages as soon as the journal entry is made. The fact that we don't see it happen obscures the process. The tradeoff for obscurity is that computer programs save countless hours spent posting entries and searching for inevitable posting errors.

There you have it: The triple-double of double-entry bookkeeping. It is a deceptively simple—but genius—system with uses far beyond what we've discussed so far. It is the foundation of accounting, finance, and economics that modern societies rely on and without which merchants would have little rest.

One last comment before we move on. From what we've discussed so far, we can develop a new appreciation for banks. Most of us think of a bank as the institution that keeps our money safe while it is in transit between transactions or as the place that either will or won't lend us money when we most need it. Both perceptions are true, but banks quietly perform another critical role that binds entire economies and societies together. It is a role we all depend on but few of us fully appreciate. We can make a credible case that the most important role of banks is to act as the world's bookkeepers. They are the trusted standard against which the quality of our books is measured and our transactions confirmed. Think about it. If you disagree about a transaction with a customer, vendor, the IRS, or anyone else, what is the first thing you do? You check with the bank to see if a payment has cleared or a deposit has been recorded. If the bank has it in its records, that's typically the end of the argument. While bookkeeping (which we'll look at in the next chapter) is the foundation of economies, banks are the cornerstones on which they rest.

CHAPTER 3

Good Decisions Depend on Good Books

 If [there is] not a good bookkeeper in your business,
you will go on groping like a blind man.

—Pacioli

W E OFTEN HEAR THE THREE WORDS *BOOKKEEPING*, *ACCOUNTING*, AND *finance* used loosely as synonyms. The three are intertwined but distinct disciplines. Bookkeeping is the practice of faithfully and accurately recording transactions. *Accounting* is the application of standards and laws (for small business, this generally means tax laws) to bookkeeping. For example, bookkeepers know *how* to record a transaction as an expense. Tax law dictates whether they *may* record it as an expense. Accounting standards, rules, and laws—unlike bookkeeping —are subject to interpretation and are forever changing. That's why accounting is best left to the professionals. *Finance* is the use of reports prepared from good books to making business decisions. Intelligent people may disagree with my definitions but all would agree that that it begins with bookkeeping.

The impact of bookkeeping, or the lack of it, on lives is very real. I cannot stress that point enough.

I received a call early one March from a woman named Carolyn. Her voice was quivering, and she was obviously distraught.

She said her banker told her to call. She and her husband, Rodney, had always had a good marriage and had worked together in their contracting business for more than 12 years. Carolyn and another woman did all the administrative work. Rodney ran operations and spent most of his time working in the field with their 14 technicians. So far, theirs sounded like a classic example of a mom-and-pop business, but she said things seemed different now.

For the last several months, they hadn't been able to pay off their credit cards and were falling behind with all their suppliers. Their receivables were down, and they had just maxed out their credit line (which was why her banker told her to call me). To top it off, they had missed two paychecks because they didn't have enough cash to pay both themselves and their employees. Carolyn's every instinct was screaming, "We're losing money!"

"Something's wrong," she said. "I told my husband we need to do something, but he won't listen to me. He just gets frustrated and mad. This last week, he even yelled at me and told me to be quiet! He's never said anything like that to me before, and we're not going to last long if he does it again."

Rodney had been bidding jobs on the cheap to get more sales and, as he put it, "to grow the business." It had worked. Their job count was up 30 percent over the previous year to date and they still had a lot of outstanding bids they might win. It was shaping up to be a record year—for work, anyway.

"Rod says that our profit and loss statement shows we're making money. He says I must be messing things up, and I just need to figure it out. I don't think I'm doing anything wrong. I think he's bidding jobs too low and he's *buying things* we can't afford. Our cash problems and the accusations going back and forth are causing a lot of stress at the office and even more at home. We hardly even talk to each other anymore."

We agreed to meet a few days later, and when we did, I asked to look at her books. Carolyn had done a great job of keeping current records in

QuickBooks.[2] When I clicked to see the profit and loss report, it showed a $55,000 net profit. Not bad for the first two months of the year for a company their size. Then I noticed something. In the upper left corner of the report were the words *cash basis*.

Hmmm…

I clicked a button in QuickBooks to produce the same report on the "accrual basis" and presto! When reported on the accrual basis, that $55,000 profit transformed into a $75,000 loss. Problem identified. Where their cash-basis report showed a profit, the accrual basis report showed they were hemorrhaging money in losses. As of this writing, it remains to be seen if they will recover. How that can happen is not the point here. We will get to that later. The point is that good people making an earnest effort to keep good books can still produce misleading reports that lead to strained relationships, bad decisions, and losses. Clearly, it is not enough to keep books. You have to keep *proper* books, and to do that, you have to know what proper books look like. With that, let's look at the three types of bookkeeping.

---

2 Carolyn kept her books current by making daily entries into QuickBooks. My experience has shown that such discipline is the exception among small businesses. As you begin to rely more on good bookkeeping information, it becomes more important to keep your books current. Proper procedures require you to make journal entries daily while transactions are fresh in mind (the computer will automatically post to the appropriate ledger pages). There are other huge benefits to daily entries: They improve cash flow through prompt billing and they reduce the chance that you'll forget to invoice a customer! (If you've never failed to invoice a customer, you are the exception.)

CHAPTER 4

Three Types of Bookkeeping

The difference between the right word and the almost right word is the difference between lightning and the lightning bug.

—MARK TWAIN

THINK ABOUT THAT. A CONTRACTOR AND HIS WIFE WORKING DILIGENTLY to keep good books couldn't answer even the first of the five questions: Are we making money? As a result, the husband continued to make bad decisions, their personal life was a wreck, and they were falling further and further behind. You can't afford to let that happen to you.

Again, don't panic. I already promised that you do not need to learn bookkeeping rules or to keep books yourself to avoid disaster, but you must be able to recognize proper books in order to insist on them for your business.

I have encountered all sorts of attempts to keep books in small businesses, but they generally fall into three categories. See if these look familiar.

The lowest form of bookkeeping is cash-basis, single-entry bookkeeping, which means we let banks keep our books for us. Such books are not worthy of the name and are not at all useful for management purposes. Cash-basis books record transactions only after they have been settled—after someone paid us or we paid someone. These books are little more than lists of payments made and deposits received. They are little more than bank statements; in fact, they very often *are* bank statements. This is one of the ways we rely on banks to keep our books for us.

A high-tech version of these books might be an Excel spreadsheet with columns of deposits and withdrawals or it might be deposits and withdrawals entered into QuickBooks with a few credit card charges thrown in to confuse things. The problem is that they can't tell you what you owe your suppliers or what you are owed by your customers, and in spite of the name "cash basis," they can't tell you where your cash went. They do a poor job of recording your inventory and reporting your net worth. Those are a lot of questions cash-basis books don't answer—heck, as we've seen, they can't even tell you if you made a profit!

Cash-basis, single-entry books are good only for paying taxes—and then only after a competent accountant works magic on them. They are better than nothing because paying taxes keeps you out of jail, but taxes are about the past and the past has passed. You can't do anything about it. Management is about the future. To be useful as a management tool, your books must provide *complete* and *current* information and present it in a way that is useful for making decisions. Cash-basis, single-entry books don't do that.[3]

The next highest form of bookkeeping is accrual-basis, double-entry bookkeeping. To paraphrase Mark Twain from above, the difference between these and the first type of books is the difference between lightning and the lightning bug. Double-entry, accrual bookkeeping records both sides of every transaction when it happens, whether or not it has been settled by payment. In small businesses, these books are generally kept in QuickBooks or equivalent software. When kept correctly, they will tell you all those things that cash-basis, single-entry books can't: What you owe, what you're owed, what you own, where your cash went, and whether you made a profit. Proper accrual-basis books tell you the correct and current score. *But* the way I usually find accounts arranged in QuickBooks, even accrual-basis, double-entry books can be improved.

---

3 We will see in chapter 19 how cash-basis books cost an owner the sale of his business.

The highest form of bookkeeping—the kind you must insist on for your business—is accrual-basis, double-entry books in which accounts have been arranged to make certain information easily available and useful for making decisions about the future. These are proper books, and we will explore them in-depth in Sections II and III.

Proper books require:

1. Double-entry

2. Accrual basis

3. Daily entries

4. Proper arrangement

I described the elements of proper books so you can recognize them and understand what you need in your role as a decision-maker. Ideally, it is not your role to set up your books. Setting up proper books generally requires a special type of accountant. I say *special* because accountants come in different varieties. To name a few, there are tax, audit, forensic, and cost accountants. Any of them *could* set up your books but tax, audit, and forensic accountants are concerned primarily with the past. For various reasons, they compile, study, and want to know what has already happened. As a decision-maker, you are not as concerned with the past as you are with the future. You are helpless when confronted with advice that begins with the phrase, "What you should have done was…"

You need to work with a good cost accountant (see chapter 22 for specifics about how to get started). By *good*, I mean someone who loves divining direction and helping to create strategies, and who can explain and refine the concepts we will discuss in this book.

Finally, to preempt a common concern that I often hear expressed, don't confuse *keeping books* on the cash basis with *paying taxes* on a cash basis. Your tax accountant may have told you that you are "on the cash basis." She is saying you *pay taxes* on the cash basis, which *does not mean you have to keep books on a cash basis.* Accountants can calculate cash-basis taxes from accrual books. They cannot create accrual-basis reports from cash books. For management purposes, there is no good reason to keep books on a cash basis.

Next, we'll see why business is so hard for most of us.

CHAPTER 5

Business Isn't Brain Surgery. It's Harder than That

What was thought to be a simple process is in fact an incredibly complicated, intricate, and complex system that I've codified and organized into a few easy-to-follow rules that are more difficult to implement than you'd think.

—MARK ANDERSON, *ANDERTOONS*

B USINESS IS AT LEAST AS COMPLEX AS BRAIN SURGERY. THE CONSEQUENCES of a business mistake may not be as abrupt or immediately serious as a slip of the scalpel but the likelihood of making mistakes in business is far greater than in brain surgery. That's because of the lack of training for business owners coupled with the complexity of business. Brain surgeons are licensed to practice medicine only after years of intense education, practice, testing, and oversight, all focused on a well-defined discipline. In contrast, business owners often begin business on a whim with no training whatsoever. An owner is licensed only after completing a few forms online and paying a $100 fee to some state agency. Because it is so easy to start a business (the World Bank reports that in 2017, it took an average of six days to create a business in the US), most business owners I've met are completely unaware of what it takes to succeed and are quickly ambushed by reality.

The reality is that there are four broad disciplines common to all businesses. We may complicate matters by adding more but there are only four. Our businesses—not us, our businesses—must deal with all four disciplines just to survive. Our businesses must be balanced and at least *good* at all of these disciplines in order to thrive. The four disciplines are:

- Guiding the business
- Getting the business
- Doing the business
- Administering the business

Guiding the business involves leadership. Guidance includes articulating a compelling vision for people to believe in. It includes creating and maintaining a culture consistent with our values and the vision of the company. Guidance also includes insisting on organization, setting goals, creating plans, holding people accountable, providing incentives, delegating duties and responsibilities, and more. Many business owners—probably a majority of those I've met—have heard of these topics but spend little or no time reading or thinking about them, let alone crafting and implementing activities to improve in these areas. When they do, it's usually to address a current crisis rather than to provide strategic guidance.

Getting the business involves marketing and sales. Marketing is attracting the leads; sales is closing the deal. I've never met a business owner who was unaware of the critical need for marketing and sales, but again, most of us spend little or no time acquiring skills, developing strategies, or implementing plans in either area. If you don't believe that, ask business owners how they attract customers. Most will answer, "Word of mouth." Ask them to show you their referral program or to tell you the value of a customer and the cost of acquiring one. A few will give you good answers, but most will quickly admit they don't have a referral program, a marketing strategy, or any idea of the value of a customer or the cost of acquiring one.

Doing the business is delivering on the promises made in marketing and sales. It is delivering the goods or services we sell. A large majority of small business owners are really good at just one of the four disciplines—

doing—because they started a business to deliver a product or service they understand, are passionate about, and know how to deliver. Unfortunately, a passion to deliver a product or service is not enough to thrive in business.

Administering the business involves everything else. Small business owners quickly recognize my description of administrative functions as "all those things you had never even heard of when you started your business." Administrative functions include things such as managing cash, bookkeeping, payroll, IT, HR policies, regulatory compliance, taxes, legal issues, liability insurance, workman's comp, health insurance, banking—and the list could go on for pages. Most small business owners were completely unequipped to deal with these matters when they began their businesses.

As I said above, most small business owners are really good at only one of the four disciplines of business and that one is "doing." The occasional new business will be good at two: Doing and getting. An unbalanced business that is good at only one or two of the four disciplines might survive but is always in peril. A business that can deliver but can't sell will fail. A business that can sell but can't deliver will fail. A business that can sell and deliver but runs out of cash, falls behind on taxes, or lets their insurance lapse the month before an accident will fail. And, of course, a business without leadership and purpose, a defined culture and standards, and planning and goals has little chance of selling, delivering, *or* managing over the long haul and will fail. Your business must be at least *good* at all four disciplines in order to thrive.

Those are harsh assertions but they're true. An unbalanced approach to business largely explains why half of all businesses fail within five years and why half of the survivors fail before 10 years. It also explains why only 4 percent of the 30 million businesses in the United States ever reach $1 million in sales, a mere fraction of 1 percent of small businesses ever reach $10 million in sales, and 80 percent of small businesses never hire even a single employee.[4] As an owner confronting those statistics, you can clearly see the importance of striking a balance among the four disciplines.

When it comes to creating balance, the good news is that there are only four disciplines. The bad news is that there are a lot of particulars within each. It is not likely that you, as an owner, can become an expert in all of them but your business can. Like a brain surgeon who relies on a team of anesthesiologists, skilled nurses, and equipment specialists, you can rely on a team of skilled employees and advisors such as bookkeepers, CPAs, marketing pros, IT and HR experts, bankers, lawyers, insurance agents, and so on.[5]

Bookkeeping and financial reporting is largely an administrative function, and by that, I mean someone in administration usually keeps the books and produces the reports. However, bookkeeping information is critical to every discipline in business. The individuals performing any function of business need to know how they did and what to do in the future. Bookkeeping provides the historic scorecard and informs future decisions.

Leaders need financial information to measure performance of their companies and the people in it, to forecast cash needs, to plan for growth, to set goals as an objective means to hold people accountable, to provide incentives, and, as we will see throughout this book, to inform virtually every decision they make.

Sales and marketing people need numbers to help measure the effects of their efforts. The information provides an objective means to determine conversion rates, the value of a customer, and the cost of acquiring a customer. The information is invaluable to those of us who want to systematically and deliberately increase the return on our marketing and sales efforts.

People in production need numbers. They need to know if they are producing efficiently, whether they should add or drop a product or service,

---

4 This is an improvement over the 80 perfect failure rate you may have heard about. Source: "SBA Frequently Asked Questions: Small Business, 2018," accessed December 2, 2019, https://www.sba.gov/sites/default/files/advocacy/Frequently-Asked-Questions-Small-Business-2018.pdf.
5 And, of course, business coaches.

whether they should change their prices, buy a new machine, or expand the plant. Again, the numbers report the effects of past decisions and inform decisions about the future.

As we will see in our discussion about breakeven in chapter 14, we can use numbers to inform virtually every decision in business. Before we do that, we have to be clear about the purpose of business and why numbers matter.

CHAPTER 6

The Purpose of Business and Why Numbers Matter

Results have to be measurable. In the end, you have to be able to look and without any argument answer the question, "Did we do it?" Yes or no. Simple, with no judgment.

—ANDY GROVE, COFOUNDER OF INTEL

ALL BUSINESS MATTERS CAN BE GROUPED INTO TWO BROAD CATEGORIES: The subjective and the objective. Subjective matters involve activities and behaviors. In many respects, subjective matters *are* your business because they are what you do and how you do it. The subjective group includes some hard-to-define matters such as motives, leadership, vision, value, selling, teamwork, quality, marketing, incentive, purpose, satisfaction, and so on. All of those are subjective because there are infinite definitions of each, yet only fuzzy definitions of ideal outcomes. Deciding which approach is best for your business or how well you performed at, say, prospecting for sales is largely a matter of opinion. To illustrate this, suppose that you and your sales manager disagree about how sales are going. She feels good about sales; you don't. Who is right is a matter of opinion—unless one of you brings data to support your position, in which case you have crossed over to the objective side.

Objective business matters involve numbers. They are important because they are the score. Numbers were created (or discovered, if you prefer) to measure things. That's at least a large part of what they do. They provide feedback on what we've done and, as we will see, they also provide guidance for the future.

Imagine playing a game without keeping score. Really take a moment and imagine a basketball game with no score. You, your team, your opponent, and the fans would be lost. Or, more likely, each would find his or her own way to keep score and each player would find a separate way to pursue their own goals. Implied in Andy Grove's quote about results is that you cannot manage what you do not measure. If you don't manage, everything that happens to you—good or bad—is an accident. You might thrive by accident but it's not likely.

Measurement is the result of defining and quantifying important indicators and describing the results as numbers. Numbers are valuable because they are objective and independent of opinion. They are the dispassionate arbiter that tells us what we need to know, regardless of whether we want to know or how we *feel* about it. Financial reports, and this book, are about managing the process of objectively using numbers to guide you.

People frequently ask me which is more important, the subjective or objective. I respond with a question of my own, "Which is more important, your heart or your lungs?" (That's a rhetorical question, of course, but I've had a surprising number of people try to make the case for one over the other!) My point is that we need both.

Most small business owners are really good at something, usually something subjective. They are good at sales, innovation, retailing, design, customer service, company culture, for instance. In contrast, I rarely encounter small business owners who are really good at using numbers to guide their decisions.

There are many subjective reasons for going into business. All are valid and they vary from owner to owner. There is only one purely objective reason and it is true for every business. The single, objective purpose of business is to turn cash into more cash.[6] That's it.

Notice that I didn't say "to increase sales" or "to make a profit." Business owners often obsess about sales or profit (surprisingly, more often about sales than profit) and neglect the rest of the business cycle set out in the following illustration. That's a mistake because you can't pay your bills with sales, you can't make payroll with profit, and you can't meet your subjective goals if you're broke. All of those things require cash, which brings us to the objective business cycle.

Take a look at this illustration, and let's run through the business cycle from beginning to end.

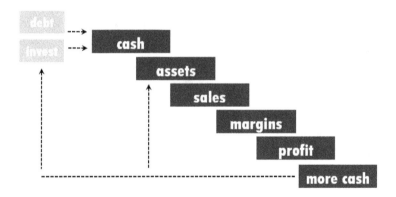

---

6 Businesses pay us cash in two ways. The first comes from the profits of operating a business. The second comes when we sell our business and convert equity value into cash. Most small business owners have not even considered this second source of cash, even though it has the potential to exceed the cash produced from operations. We will look at this second source of cash in chapter 19.

The Business Cycle

You need cash to start a business, and there are two ways to get it: Debt and investment. Debt, of course, means you borrow the cash. Investment means that you or someone else puts up cash in exchange for ownership. Whatever the original source, the illustration shows that you use the cash to buy assets—things like real estate, equipment, and inventory—which you use to generate sales, which lead to margins (the critically important difference between sales and the cost of sales, which we will discuss in-depth in chapters 10 and 14), which lead to profit, which leads back to cash. Because of profit, you end with more cash than you started with. You use the ending cash to repay debt, to pay a return on investment, or to buy more assets to keep the cycle going.

That's the idea, anyway. In reality, cash gets stuck or leaks out at every stage. Very often, cash barely trickles out the bottom even though the owner continues to pour it in at the top. It doesn't take long to get too much of that!

Imbalances involving sales, margins, accounts receivable, and inventory are among the most common ways cash either gets stuck or leaks out of the business cycle. But that's not true for all businesses. Owners who understand and pay attention to the full cycle get very good at it. Some are so good that they generate more cash than profit.[7]

For every action we take at any step in the cycle, we must consider the effect on subsequent steps. We must know that:

- Assets efficiently lead to sales.

- Sales minus the cost of goods sold lead to adequate margins.

- Margins after overhead lead to profit.

---

7 Some owners can generate more cash than profit because of depreciation and amortization expenses. As you will see in Sections II and III, depreciation and amortization are noncash expenses that reduce profit but do not consume cash.

- Profits will quickly convert to cash.

- Sufficient cash is available to sustain us through every stage of the cycle.

That's the purpose of numbers and financial statements. There are three standard financial statements because that's how many it takes to cover the entire cycle. Each report has a different purpose and covers different parts of the cycle, but taken together, they show us how well we are progressing from one stage to the next through the entire cycle. They can show us where cash gets stuck and where the leaks are. Armed with that information, we can focus our efforts on resolving specific problems rather than exhausting ourselves fighting a general feeling of angst.

Owners who understand the full cycle of business consider every step of the cycle in every decision. They don't chase sales for the sake of sales, they don't tie up their cash in excess inventory, they don't compete by reducing their prices, they don't let their accounts receivable threaten their businesses, and they don't squander cash buying things they don't need to "save on taxes." As a result, they lead more productive and less stressful lives than their peers.

Even if we fully understand and appreciate the cycle of business, we may have to overcome subconscious beliefs in order to be effective.

CHAPTER 7

Beware Your Unexamined Beliefs

He thinks in secret and it comes to pass, reality is but his looking glass.

—JAMES ALLEN, *As a Man Thinketh*

M AYBE YOU AGREE WITH EVERYTHING YOU'VE READ SO FAR. IT MAKES sense but what do you do? How do you *behave*? The answers to those questions largely depend on what you believe.

When I speak before groups about beliefs, I often begin by asking them to describe a salesperson. I usually hear descriptions such as *pushy*, *obnoxious*, *liars*, *sleazy*, and *annoying*. I follow their answers by asking who in the room makes a living from sales. They are usually on to me by then and every hand in the room eventually goes up. The purpose of the question is to illustrate the impact your beliefs have on your actions. No wonder so many people hate selling—especially cold-calling. Who wants to be included among the annoying, sleazy liars of the world?

I use salespeople to illustrate the power of beliefs because many of us have similar beliefs about salespeople but we also have powerful beliefs about money and business. Those beliefs determine our behaviors and actions.

An unpleasant experience I had with a former employee shows how beliefs directly affect behaviors and lives.

"Are you sitting down?" It was our newest regional salesman, Frank, talking to a customer on the phone. "I've got pricing for you, and I just want to be sure you're sitting down when I tell you." I was in Georgia to find out why Frank was struggling, and it was apparent. He was on the telephone delivering a quote for a small commercial job—the price was less than one-fifth our average sale—but Frank thought the $10,000 price was a lot of money. It showed. *Are you sitting down?*

Are you kidding me? My head almost exploded as I listened to him prattle on and on trying to justify the "high price" to the customer. He planted the idea that our bid was too high, and he drove the point home with his misguided efforts to explain it. Frank's beliefs directly affected us both. We lost the sale and, despite my efforts to change his thinking, Frank lost his job.

Beliefs are those things we hold to be true based on the evidence we've gathered thus far. Beliefs begin when we accept our interpretation of a circumstance, event, or comment as true and representative without challenging our subconscious assumptions about it. Someone who grows up in a poor family and hears every day, "It's too expensive," "We can't afford it," or "Nice things are for rich people" starts to believe that money is precious, scarce, and a source of pain. They begin, consciously or not, to accumulate evidence to support the belief.

This is what happened to Frank. His beliefs about money led to comments such as "Are you sitting down?" which led to lost sales, which led to his unemployment, which, I am sure, reinforced his belief that money was the root cause of his troubles.

Beliefs are hard to change because they live in our subconscious. We are not even aware of them. However, once identified, we can undo a belief by reversing the process through which it was formed. Once aware, we can look for and gather contrary evidence that challenges the old belief and reinforces a new one.

Some of us may have benefited from a mentor or from exceedingly good native judgment so we begin at a sophisticated level of understanding, but many of us pass through a predictable series of beliefs.

People who are new to business (and many who are not) believe that selling is the most important activity in business. I see that notion reinforced at every sales seminar I attend and in every book I read about sales:

"It all starts with sales!"

"Sales professionals are the point of the spear!"

"Salespeople are 'rainmakers!'"[8]

All because the salesperson can sell. If you believe that, go back and read through the four disciplines of business above. A company with great sales is dead if it can't produce and deliver a product, if it runs out of cash, if it runs afoul of labor law, or if it lacks a compelling vision. Sales are critical but they are only *one* of the four critical disciplines of business.

If we believe sales are the most important activity in business, our actions and behaviors will match our belief. We will concentrate our time and energy on sales to the detriment of the other disciplines of business and stages of the business cycle (and if we also believe that salespeople are sleazy, we will be miserable doing it).

The following stories about The Wannabe Boss and the Tenderfoot Business Owner illustrate the thinking of people stuck on sales, and it's easy to see how thinking affects performance.

---

8 I've seen business owners put up with behavior from salespeople that they wouldn't tolerate at home from a three-year-old. They are absolutely terrified at the thought of losing sales, even if it means tolerating behaviors that can destroy the cultures of their companies.

The Wannabe Boss

A friend of mine manages the local branch of a regional bank. She told me a story that shows how a true wannabe boss thinks about sales, money, and the cycle of business.

A man walked into her office still wearing his chef's uniform from a local restaurant. As he plopped into the chair across from her desk, he said he needed to borrow some money.

"What for?" my friend asked.

"I want to start my own restaurant," he answered.

"Are you sure? The restaurant business can be pretty tough."

"Yeah, I'm sure," he said. "I'm tired of working for someone else. The man I work for *made over $1 million last year*, but I did all the work."

My friend had to choke back her reaction. She recognized the logo on his uniform, and it just so happened that she was the restaurant's loan officer. A week earlier, she had defended the owner in a loan committee meeting to keep the bank from calling in his note. The chef was right that the restaurant brought in $1 million *in sales*. What he didn't know was that it had lost money doing it. To the chef, "making money" meant sales. The naïve fellow didn't have a clue about business, let alone the objective purpose of business. My friend told him she would look at his idea after he brought her some cost projections, but she never saw him again.

If you have any doubts that someone could be that clueless, ask the next employee you see how much money his or her company "makes." If they have any idea at all, the answer they give will most likely be sales, not profit.

The Tenderfoot Business Owner

There is something macho about sales. A second banker referred me to Chris, a paving contractor who was obsessed with sales. He was fond of mentioning how many millions he had sold the prior year. He never mentioned profit because he didn't know whether or not he made a profit. When we met, Chris didn't have even a basic understanding of margins or what it took to earn a profit. His books were in shambles. They were improperly arranged and were months behind. I doubt he would have had any books at all if his bank hadn't required them.

Because he had no proper books, Chris didn't know his costs or margins. He didn't know whether he made gross profit on jobs or how much he had to sell to cover his overhead expenses. His only criterion for pricing jobs was to "get the work." He defended that philosophy with comments such as "If I get the sale, I can find a way to keep some of the money," "I need the work to keep the guys busy," and "I need to keep the cash coming in to pay the bills." His pursuit of sales without margins was futile, and it was leading him toward disaster.

After suffering loss after loss and under pressure from cash shortages and the bank, he called me. We worked to improve his understanding of the sales cycle. He agreed with the concepts in theory, but it was a long and hard struggle to convince him that it was better to lose bids with negative margins than it was to win them. He began to take smaller jobs with higher margins. He could no longer brag about his sales numbers but he had positive margins and, as of this writing, he has finally begun to make a small profit.

If you are to advance beyond a preoccupation with sales, you must fully grasp the idea that sales alone are not enough. You have to earn margins and profits in order to survive but even profitable companies cannot survive without cash.

The Blistered Business Owner

I received a call from a business owner in February a few years ago. It was obvious he was desperate and near the end of his rope. He had opened a new business the previous July with $30,000 in savings. The business sold fixtures to builders and by the time we talked, he was selling more than $100,000 of merchandise per month. Going from zero to $100,000 per month in seven months is a good thing, right? Not this time. He called me because he was on the verge of a breakdown. His was a clear case of an owner who was hung up on the last step in the business cycle: converting profit to cash.

When he opened his business, he concentrated on sales but he also had a good grasp of margins and showed a nice profit on his accrual-basis books. So why the meltdown? Because he was almost completely out of cash. Suppliers had him on credit hold, which delayed his orders, which had customers complaining. One customer was even threatening to sue him. He was under constant pressure and was taking a lot of phone calls from customers. Very few of them were good.

How did it happen? He sold goods in a hard-nosed industry with well-funded competitors who used their 60- to 90-day credit terms as a competitive weapon. His lust for sales compelled him to match their terms.

His merchandise cost him 60 cents of each sales dollar and all his sales were "on account," which meant the customer wouldn't pay him for at least 60 days. That meant that for every dollar increase in sales from one month to the next, he needed another 60 cents to finance the cost of the sale. The higher the sales, the worse the problem. By the time he called me, he had over $250,000 in accounts receivable, about $140,000 in past due bills, but only $10,000 cash in the bank. We got this man an SBA loan, which enabled him to continue in business. However, because his reputation had been damaged and because his nerves were so frayed, he is no longer in business. It all could have been avoided with proper planning, financing, and a disciplined sales strategy as we will see when we meet him again in chapter 15.

You may be thinking, "Hey, that's kind of obvious. Everybody knows you have to manage accounts receivable." Maybe so, but cash problems due to accounts receivable are as common as grass on the prairie. Business owners who don't fully appreciate the last step in the cycle are often obsessed with sales and profit and ignore the last step until it's too late.

The Calloused Business Owner

Not everyone is suffering. Some have mastered the entire cycle of business, even if they don't think of their mastery in those terms. Take, for example, Michael, a contractor whose company builds concrete structures for a narrow, specialized market.

One of the first things I do when working with new clients is look at their books, including their balance sheets. The idea is first to see if they *have a balance sheet* and, if they do, to get a quick idea of the health of the business. When I clicked on Michael's balance sheet, I was staggered. The company had the equivalent of half a year's *sales* as cash in the bank (millions of dollars)! This is a rare occurrence. I asked him how it had happened.

"We're really good at what we do," he responded. "We've built a great reputation, and we protect it vigorously. Our reputation includes exceptional quality products and support, but we also protect our reputation for not being cheap. I tell our customers I have to charge them enough to take care of them. If people don't want to pay our price, they can go elsewhere."

"I understand that you charge more and are worth it," I replied, "but how do you account for all of this cash?"

As if the millions of dollars in his bank account weren't enough, his response convinced me I was talking to a seasoned, confident, and insightful business owner. "Well," he began, "as I see it, quality and service are our responsibility. We owe that to our customers, and we make sure we provide it. Their responsibility is to pay us. In the early years, I had trouble with that because I was so worried about money that I believed everyone else would be too. I was straight-up scared to ask for advance deposits because I thought it would make us look weak.

"We were acting like a bank. I finally suffered enough that I decided to put a stop to it, one way or another. We were going to end the suffering by either solving our cash problem or by going out of business. Turns out it wasn't a big deal. We started to require cash deposits before beginning work and progress payments as we go along. We have never spent more on a job than the customer has paid us. The customer's final payment to us is basically for our profit [margin]."

The stages of a business owners' evolution generally align with the three financial statements. Those who believe sales are most important devote their attention to the top line of the income statement. Those who have advanced to the next stage look farther down the income statement to manage their margins and profits. Those who have learned to believe in managing assets and cash pay attention to the balance sheet and the statement of cash flows. That's a natural progression in the evolution of business owners with experience, education, insight, necessity, and suffering providing the incentive to advance from one stage to the next.

The Master

There is a fourth, very select group of business owners who have advanced to think differently from the rest of us. Rather than concentrating solely on profits and cash, they concentrate on increasing the value of the business itself. This group focuses on the balance sheet.

It may surprise you—it surprised me—but most of the business owners I've met don't believe their businesses have value, at least not more than the value of their real estate, equipment, and inventory. I know because I've asked countless business owners what their businesses are worth. "Who would want it?" is the answer I hear most often. That response is the hallmark of surrender coming from harried business owners who are tired of the fight. They are so exhausted from the daily grind that they can't imagine someone wanting to take over their roles.

This select group of master business owners, however, has learned to focus on opportunity. They understand that their businesses have value, even if the value is only the untapped opportunity to grow and improve. They know they can increase the value of a business dramatically by understanding what businesses buyers want and how they determine the value of a business.

These owners, like the rest of us, benefit from sales, margins, profit, and cash but they don't think of those things as reasons to be in business. They think of them as tools they can use to increase the value of the business itself. While most of us work hard to earn 10, 20, or maybe even 30 percent of sales as net profits, they work to increase the value of the company by hundreds or even 1,000 percent in a few short years. They benefit from profits while they own the business and then pocket a fortune when they sell it. This type of thinking is normally the domain of hedge funds and private equity firms that not only believe but also know it can be done.

The main differences between a master business owner, such as a hedge fund manager, and the typical business owner is their thinking. A master's thinking, strategies, and methods are available to all of us who are open to learn, as we will see in chapter 19.

CHAPTER 8

In Defense of Profit

I been rich and I been poor, and believe you me, rich is better.

—Pearl Bailey

WE'VE COVERED A LOT OF TOPICS THAT AFFECT PROFIT AND CASH BUT there is a final, critical prerequisite to increasing profits—desire. It will not matter how well you keep books, how well you master the four areas of business, or how skilled you become at the methods we'll discuss in the following chapters if you do not earnestly and sincerely *want* higher profits. You have to believe it is more than just okay to increase your profit. You must believe it is the necessary, right, and proper thing to do.

You may be thinking, "Are you crazy? Of course it's right and proper to increase profit! That's the whole point of business." On the one hand, if that's how you think, read on. The following arguments may be useful if you ever need to defend your position. On the other hand, if you harbor even a hint of reluctance, unease, or doubt about profit, read on. The following arguments may dissuade you from some beliefs that are holding you back and threatening your future.

"For me, it's not about the money." A new client and I were talking about how to increase profits dramatically.

"What do you mean?" I asked.

"Business should be about being an example, it should be about responsibility and citizenship and providing for employees and doing no harm," he said.

"I agree, but you have to make a profit to be and do all of those things," I replied.

"Well, yes, I understand that, but I don't want to be greedy and make too much."

"So how much is too much?"

I didn't get an answer. I never do. I know that some people (hopefully a small minority) are put off by my constant emphasis on making money. I know that because, as a business coach, I have talked with hundreds of small business owners about profit and have had more than a few conversations like the one above. It's as if the business owners feel guilty about making a profit or feel it's somehow noble to loathe money.

I believe all the negative comments and feelings about profit are sincere but misguided. They are misguided because that sort of thinking can do great damage not only to their businesses but also to the well-being of others—great damage that is precisely the opposite of intended virtue. As Dan S. Kennedy said in his book, *No B.S. Price Strategy*, "If you live the ultimate failure of deriving less profit than possible, you do not win a merit badge for reduction of greed by self-restraint. There is no such merit badge, as the act is without merit."

Profit is not just good, it is a moral imperative. It is our duty to ourselves *and to others* to make all the money we can without resorting to coercion, lying, cheating, or stealing. Let me say that last part again so I don't have to repeat it in every section below—*without resorting to coercion, lying, cheating, or stealing.*

Here are some things to consider about profit:

1. Profit is an objective reason for business. It doesn't have to be your reason for living.

2. Everybody must make a profit. Everybody.

3. The feelings of guilt and greed are based on a fallacy.

4. Profit is a measure of our service to others.

5. Our customers have choices.

6. Profit is not cash.

7. Profit improves the world.

8. Profit is a prerequisite to altruism.

First, as we have seen, earning profit is the *objective* reason for being in business. How to use the profits is (or should be) up to the person who earned them. You can give them away if you want to. Profit makes it possible to stay in business and to continue to serve.

Second, everybody makes a profit, even those who denounce it loudly. We all intuitively, if not explicitly, know that, and we all behave accordingly. If you earn less at your job than it costs you to get there, you will stop going to work even if you want to keep going. You have to recover your costs in order to pay for your commute, and you have to make a profit to support yourself outside work. The same applies to people who don't work but are paid anyway. If it costs you more to pick up a government or retirement check than the check is worth, you would not bother to do it. Everybody *who is capable* must make a profit. Everybody. The alternative is to live off profits someone else earned.

Third, the word *greed* conjures up echoes of a common fallacy. The fixed-pie fallacy is the idea that there is a fixed amount of wealth; therefore, if someone has money, someone else must do without. The supply of money, wealth, and profit does not come from a fixed pie but rather from an abundant source. The evidence is everywhere around us.[9] The fact that you earn a profit does not hinder another person's ability to also make a profit. The clear-thinking author Dan S. Kennedy said it well, "Go to the ocean with a bucket or a teaspoon; the ocean doesn't care," and neither will your choice affect the other people on the beach. You do not need to worry about your motives either. As Adam Smith famously pointed out in his book, *The Wealth of Nations* (1776), "It is not from the benevolence of the butcher, the brewer, or the baker that we expect our dinner, but from their regard for their own interests." As we will see in the next paragraph, our seemingly selfish efforts to earn profits benefit others far more than they benefit us.

Fourth, profit is a measure of how much your contributions exceed your consumption. A woman who earns large profits, whatever her motives, cannot do so without benefiting others more than herself. This is true because *everybody's expense is somebody else's income*. What you spend as expense is income to the person you paid. Let me explain.

The average small business in the United States makes a net profit before taxes of around seven cents for each dollar of sales. We'll use 10 cents to make the math easier. That means that a business made a 10-cent profit on $1.00 of sales spent 90 cents of each sales dollar to pay expenses, for example, to a supplier. That 90 cents is income to the supplier. The supplier then spends 90 cents of each dollar it receives to pay *its* expenses to *its* suppliers. This flow of money from one business to the next is the so-called cycle of economic impact.

You		Your Supplier		Supplier's Supplier		And so on...	
Sales	$100						
Expense	90	Sales	$90				
Profit	**$10**	Expense	81	Sales	$81		
		Profit	**$9**	Expense	73	Sales	$73
				Profit	**$8**	Expense	66
						Profit	**$7**

9 For evidence of this fact, read "More From Less" by MIT professor Andrew McAfee and "The Rational Optimist" by Oxford professor Matt Ridley

The cycle of economic impact[10] continues until the effect eventually disappears at 10 times the original business' profit of 10 cents. That means that in order to generate his 10-cent profit, the original business owner helped others generate about one dollar of profit, or 10 times *more profit than it earned for itself.* If you truly want to benefit the world around you, go make money!

Fifth, profit is validation that you have served your customers, yourself, and society in general. You cannot make a profit unless your customers *choose* to do business with you. They will not choose to do business with you unless they value your offer more than they value their money.

Sixth, profit is not cash. The word *profit* conjures up images of greedy business owners driving black sedans and living lavish lives on profits wrested from vulnerable customers and produced by the efforts of underpaid employees. That is a common belief, but is it true?

To answer the question, I refer you to the subtitle of this book: "They say I make money, so why don't I have any?" You can find examples of people living large on profits but they are a minority among business owners. Profits are not cash. In fact, profits are not often available to business owners because they are tied up in the assets required to create jobs and produce goods and services. It's difficult to find global statistics on the subject, but my experience has shown that the profits in many small businesses are tied up entirely by just one asset—accounts receivable. In other words, instead of spending their profits on lavish lifestyles, business owners lend them to customers as accounts receivable in order to generate sales to keep the business cycle turning.[11] Add to that the cash invested in real estate, inventory, equipment, and other assets necessary to sustain a business, and many business owners begin to question how they will *ever* benefit from profit.

---

10 The cycle of economic impact is more complicated than this. The money we make as profit often reenters the economic cycle and some money is saved or "consumed" and does not reenter the cycle. However, the general principle holds that we cannot do well without benefiting others more than ourselves.

11 A representative of an international bank that insures accounts receivable told me that accounts receivable comprise 40% of all the assets owned by small businesses in the US.

Seventh, businesses that make "too much money" attract competition. Competition drives down prices and increases innovation, options, quality, and availability of product. (In fact, keeping prices artificially low to defend against competition is, in many situations, against the law!) Competitive innovation also forces obsolescence, which directs resources to new, more productive, and more valuable uses.

Eighth, and finally, if you don't make it, you can't give it away. Whatever your subjective motives for being in business, you have no capacity to fulfill them unless you make a profit. Even the most altruistic among us must do well in order to do good.

SECTION II

FINANCIAL STATEMENTS EXPLAINED WITHOUT NUMBERS OR MATH

CHAPTER 9

Three Reports,
Five Definitions

[We] need to bring knowledge to bear on the present, not to mention the future.

—THE DAILY DRUCKER BY PETER F. DRUCKER
WITH JOSEPH A MACIARIELLO

M OST OF US IN BUSINESS BEGAN WITH VERY LITTLE OR NO UNDERSTAND-
ing of financial statements. Forty-six years of experience working
with my own and other small businesses convinced me that the typical small
business owner has only a vague idea of what financial statements are and
even less of an idea of what to do with them. What most business owners
know is that their accountants need financial statements to keep them out of
trouble with tax authorities and bankers need them for who knows what. As
a result of not knowing, they suffer from the restlessness and uneasy minds
Pacioli describes and we've all experienced.

It's understandable that we don't know much about financial statements.
Why would we? We saw earlier in the four disciplines of business that most
of us started business to do something we're really good at and that wasn't
bookkeeping or financial statements. The ideas of bookkeeping, accounting,
and financial statements never crossed our minds beyond a haunting feeling
that there was something out there we should know more about but don't.

Accounting and finance are complex. People get PhDs in the subjects and then there are constantly changing tax rules that dictate how we record the transactions that affect our financial statements. Are we supposed to run a business and learn all that? No. We're going to leave the technical stuff to the pros and learn to use the information they provide us in financial reports to make better business decisions. That's what the reports are for. It's not effortless but neither is it very hard to learn how to use them. I know because I've done it myself without any formal training, and I've seen others do it time after time. The payoffs for our efforts are better decisions, more money, and peace of mind.

In this section, we are going to describe standard financial reports and see what they can tell us. We are not going to use any numbers or math (yet) so that we can concentrate on the form and purpose of each report.

There are three standard financial reports:

1. Income statement

2. Balance sheet

3. Statement of cash flows

There are three reports because that's how many it takes to answer five critical questions:

1. "Are we making money?"

2. "What do we own?"

3. "What do we owe?"

4. "What's left over for us?"

5. "Where did our cash go?"

The income statement answers the question "Are we making money?"

The balance sheet answers the questions "What do we own?" and "What do we owe?" and "What's left over for us?"

The statement of cash flows answers the question "Where did our cash go?"

Answers to those five questions tell us much of what we need to know about how our businesses performed in the past and where we stand today. In Section III, we will take it one question further and learn how to use financial reports to help us make decisions about the *future*.

Before we get to the reports themselves, we need to define a few financial terms. Financial terms are often used loosely such as when a manager says, "My people are my greatest *assets*" or when people talk about "cost" or "making a profit on a sale," so it's worth the time to define what *I* mean when I use them.

The three financial statements are organized by accounts. Perhaps, surprisingly, there are only five types of accounts and you've probably heard of them all:

1. Assets

2. Liabilities

3. Equity

4. Income

5. Expense

An asset is something we, or our businesses, *own* (which is why people aren't really assets). Some assets are tangible, such as inventory, trucks, equipment, and real estate. Others are intangible, such as cash in the bank, accounts receivable, and quaint assets that occasionally appear on our balance sheets with names, such as *goodwill, intellectual property rights*, or *franchise rights*.

A liability is something we, or our businesses, *owe* to people or entities outside the business. Who among us isn't familiar with accounts payable, credit card debt, vehicle loans, and mortgages? Those are all liabilities, and they are all intangible. We often *feel* debt, as when we worry and lose sleep over it, but we can't *touch* it.

Equity is *our share*. It's what the business owes to the owners. *Net equity*, also known as *net worth*, is the difference between what the business owns and what it owes to all nonowners. Net equity is what's left over for us after the business pays everybody else what it owes them.

Income, or sales, is money paid to us (or promised to us) as a result of our *selling goods and services*. It does not include money that comes into our companies from bank loans or that we, or our investors, put into the company—just sales.

Expense is money paid out by the business (or our promise to pay it later) in the *effort to get sales*. We also spend money to buy assets to get sales but that money is not an expense. We'll see the difference between an expense and an asset in the next paragraph.

There is one more term we need to get straight, and this is a good place to do it. We will often hear the word *cost* thrown around in business. Although cost is not a type of account such as the five listed above, it is an important concept. A cost is an outlay of money (or a promise to pay it later) made in anticipation of a *future benefit*. In business, that benefit is something or some action that will result in sales and profit. If the benefit of the cost is *used up in the current accounting* period, such as a month or a year, it is an expense for that period. If the benefit of the cost is *not used up in the current accounting period*, the cost is an asset. For example, the cost of a gallon of gas burned while driving to see a customer is an expense. The cost of the truck that burned the gas is an asset. A portion of the truck will be used up (it will lose a portion of its value) in every accounting period and that fact is acknowledged by a type of expense known as *depreciation*. Depreciation is a special kind of expense that we will explore further when we discuss the balance sheet, the statement of cash flows, and business valuation.

With that information, let's take a look at the income statement, which answers the question "Are we making money?" (That would be good to know, right?)

CHAPTER 10

The Income Statement: "Are We Making Money?"

You wicked and slothful servant...you ought therefore to have deposited my money with the bankers, and at my coming I should have received back my own with interest.

—Matthew 25:26–27 (WEBBE), The Parable of the Talents

O F THE THREE FINANCIAL REPORTS, THE INCOME STATEMENT IS THE most familiar to business owners, although they might call it a "profit and loss statement" or a "P&L." It's the report that answers the most fundamental question in business: *Are we making money?* We're starting with the income statement first because it's the easiest report to understand and because, above all else, we must know whether we're making money. If we're not, we have to fix that pronto—before attempting to grow, develop new products, or chase any of the myriad distractions that compete for our attention.

We must know we are selling things for more than they cost us; if not, we have to know why and we have to do something about it. Our businesses might survive over the short term on money supplied by the owners or lent to us by suppliers, banks, or credit cards, but long-term survival ultimately depends on making money. As we will see in chapter 14, the income statement is the most tactical of the three financial reports. It's the report business owners use most frequently to make and track operating decisions that directly affect profitability.

I have never met a business owner who hadn't at least attempted to create an income statement. The attempt might have been scribbles on a napkin, entries in an Excel spreadsheet, or a collection of bank statements showing deposits and withdrawals. It might have been nothing more than mental gymnastics performed entirely in our heads. Regardless of how we do it, we all seem to understand the need to compare income to expense to see if we made a profit. Despite that fact, I estimate most small business owners don't know how much money they made—or even *if* they made money—last month, last quarter, or last year! Among those who say they know, many really don't. Instead, they are reporting on gut feelings that arise from bank account balances and ballpark estimates of accounts receivable, accounts payable, inventory, and other accounts. If that seems as implausible to you as it once did to me, ask yourself, "Do I *really* know if I made money last month, and if so, how much?" Do you see what I mean?

For an income statement to be useful, it's not enough to just *try* to create one. You must get it right. As we saw with Carolyn and Rodney, the contractor couple we met in chapter 3, bad information can be more damaging than no information. On the one hand, if you don't have an income statement, at least you know that you don't know. On the other hand, if you rely on an inaccurate income statement, what you think you know is wrong and can lead to damaging decisions. In the case of Carolyn and Rodney, the misleading information led to decisions that very nearly ruined both their business and their marriage.

The consequences of Carolyn and Rodney's situation were exceptionally harsh, but their misleading income statement was hardly an exception. Most small businesses have misleading income statements for one or two common reasons. The first is cash-basis bookkeeping, which we looked at in chapter 4, and the second is the matching principle, which we'll define shortly.

Cash-Basis Bookkeeping

The first problem is cash-basis bookkeeping. Recall that cash-basis bookkeeping means we record transactions only after they have been settled by payment—in other words, after someone paid us or we paid someone else. This is the problem that tripped up Carolyn and her husband. Carolyn prepared her income statement on the cash basis. At the time I met her, her cash-basis income statement showed a $55,000 profit for the first quarter of the year. The same report prepared on the accrual basis—which records transactions when they *occur* rather than when they are *paid*—showed a $75,000 loss, which was a $130,000 swing to the negative.

How exactly did that happen? In their case, customers owed the company a lot of money on January 31 of the prior year. Because they hadn't been paid yet, none of the accounts receivable appeared on her year-end, cash-basis income statement. As they collected the accounts in the first quarter of the following year, the collections started showing up as cash-basis income. What looked like impressive results for the current year were really just collections of sales made the prior year. Their problem was compounded by Rodney's bad judgment. The illusion of profit inspired his confidence, and he went on a buying spree, purchasing inventory and equipment which totally exhausted their cash.

Cash-basis accounting is a common problem because so many of us allow customers 30 days to pay us and buy from suppliers who allow us 30 days to pay them, yet we don't record any of those transactions in our cash-basis books.

Matching

The second problem is a failure to follow the matching principle. Matching is a basic accounting principle that says we must record our expenses in the same period as related income. I come across matching problems in most of the small businesses with which I work. Sometimes it's not a big deal. Many times, it is a very big deal.

Matching may sound simple (or it may not), but in practice it is confusing and hard to do properly, so I'm going to remind you again: *You* are not going to do the matching. You are going to have an accountant or quality bookkeeper do it for you. We are discussing it here so you can see why it's so important.

Matching problems arise due to one (or both) of these errors:

1. Bookkeepers record expenses before they are expenses.

2. They record sales before they are sales.

Benco was a victim of the first matching error. The manufacturing company, which makes custom and specialty farm machinery, routinely recorded expenses before they were really expenses. Benco is owned by the Benson family in a rural west Texas town. The company had been in continuous operation for 26 years when I met the family. It was then, and is now, an important employer in their town and county. Many families depend on Benco getting things right and staying in business in a tough manufacturing market.

I was excited to begin working with the Bensons because they were not familiar with breakeven or other concepts I was confident would quickly improve their efficiency and profits. After I gathered the usual introductory information from them, I asked to see their books. Just as with Carolyn and Rodney, the Bensons had long been diligent about posting entries into their bookkeeping software. All the information had been entered, but their income statement showed a significant loss for the year. I asked if they knew they were losing money.

"Oh, yes," said Mr. Benson, president of Benco. "We are always losing money, and we have been for most of the last 26 years. That's why we don't look at our income statement anymore."

I wasn't convinced they had really suffered 26 years of continual losses, so I asked him if they were constantly putting money into the business to keep it going. No. Did they constantly borrow money to keep the operation afloat? No. I then asked him how the business could possibly have survived 26 years of uninterrupted losses.

"The good Lord provides," he answered.

"Well, yes," I answered, "He does, and your books ought to reflect that fact."

Benco was obviously getting misleading information from their income statements. They kept accrual-basis books, so cash-basis bookkeeping was not their problem. After a few more questions, I found the issue to be that they recorded expenses before they were really expenses. The Benson family's 26 years of losses were really 26 years of matching problems. The company used large quantities of steel, paint, and purchased parts but did not keep track of inventory. Every time a shipment of material arrived, they immediately expensed it as cost of goods sold, which would be okay except that most of it wasn't expense. It was inventory still at the plant, stacked to the ceiling in racks and piled on pallets that covered the yard[12]. Cost of goods sold is the proper expense account for production materials but *not until they are sold*. Until then, they are inventory assets, not expenses. It is certain that, had they looked at the right times, the Bensons would have seen profitable months mixed in with the losses. But they had grown so skeptical about their income statements that they quit looking.

Another company was a victim of the second matching error: It recorded sales before they were really sales. This second type of matching error leads to similar problems but it works the other way around and overstates profit. Harold became my client about three months before I wrote this sentence. His company, H and M Designs, manufactures custom cabinetry for general contractors who work on multifamily real estate projects. He gets his business by quoting projects, and the quotes are good for 30 days. At any given time, he may have 50 quotes outstanding, totaling more than a million dollars' worth of possible work.

---

12 That much inventory is bad news for manufacturers, but it is a topic for a book on lean management.

Harold lives five states away from me so we do our weekly coaching online. During our first meeting, I asked him to send me his year-to-date financial statements. He did so promptly, which was a good sign. I opened them while still on the call and glanced at his income statement. It looked good. It appeared to be arranged properly, and it showed a $90,000 profit on $560,000 of sales for the first two months of the year. That's a net profit of 16 percent, which is above average for many small businesses and way above average for most of them. Because the profits looked good, I didn't immediately dive into his financials, and we focused our efforts on other, seemingly more urgent issues.

At the end of the following month, I asked to see the financials again. I was dismayed to see the $90,000 net profit had evaporated and in its place was a net loss of $42,000. Harold hadn't mentioned any obvious disasters to account for the dramatic swing. When I asked him to explain the difference, he couldn't. "Happens all the time," he said. "I never know what I'm going to see when I look at our profits." It took about five minutes to uncover what was going on with his books.

As with the Bensons, Harold expensed materials as soon as they arrived, but he doesn't keep a large inventory so the error didn't distort his income statement very much. His matching problem was of the second kind. He recorded sales before they were sales.

Harold had always had a hard time keeping track of the 50 or more quotes he had outstanding. To keep his won jobs separate from quotes, he immediately entered them as *invoiced sales* in his books as soon as he was awarded a contract. Let that sink in. *He immediately recorded as a sale any bid that he won as soon as he was awarded the project.* This was before he had done any work or spent a dime on materials. I trust it is apparent that this practice inflates sales. It reports all the income and none of the expense for the contracted jobs. Although most of us would say we "sold" a project when we win a bid, we understand that we cannot include in our books the income from products we haven't produced or work we haven't done. In doing so, you report all the income and none of the expense in one period, then all the expense and none of the income in a following period. It was the rise and fall in the level of overstated sales that led to a $90,000 profit one month, followed by a $42,000 loss the next. It's not surprising that Harold didn't trust his books.

Chris, the paving contractor we met in chapter 7, was a victim of combined matching errors. He both recorded his expenses before they were expenses and his sales before they were sales. What a mess!

When I first met Chris, he hadn't looked at his financial reports for months. "Why would I?" he asked when I brought up the subject. "One month I'm making money, the next month I'm losing my ass. I never know what's going on until after [way after] the end of the year when my accountant tells me whether or not I made a profit. Usually not. My banker is on my case all the time, and I have no idea what to tell him. I hate this stuff. I *hate* it."

It's easy to see how the violent swings happened. His jobs normally took longer than one month to complete. He would record expenses for material and labor used one month and then record the income when he got paid in following months. The first month looked horrible and the following months looked fantastic, but neither result was accurate. Multiply those matching errors by a large number of jobs all at different stages of completion and payment and you can understand why Chris hated bookkeeping and finance.

These few examples (I could provide many more) show that it's easy to mess up an income statement, which can lead to misinformed decisions. If you can identify with any of the examples, take heart. The income statement is not difficult once you understand the fundamentals.

The Income Statement

The income statement is a period statement, which means it tells you whether you made money over a specific period. Every income statement has a beginning date and an ending date, which typically represents the first and last days of a month, a quarter, or a year.[13] The income statement compares sales for a period to expenses for the same period. At the bottom of the report, it shows the remainder after subtracting expenses from sales. A positive remainder is profit; a negative remainder is a loss. Simple, right? Well…yes and no.

The income statement and the arithmetic are simple, but as the above examples show, income statements can report wildly different results for the same period, depending on how they are prepared. To be sure we have an accurate, useful report, we have to understand what information goes into it and why it matters.

Most of the income statements in small businesses start out looking like the one below. There are usually more accounts than in the example, and the names of the items may be different but the structure is the same:

---

13 If you use QuickBooks or similar software, you'll see that it asks you for "from" and "to" dates to define the period you want your income statement to cover.

a lot of them, and we've already seen the two most dangerous ones: Cash-basis bookkeeping and the matching principle. The problems that Carolyn, Benco, Harold, and Chris encountered show clearly that you can't afford to get the details wrong.

I've noticed that six issues cause most of the problems. You may encounter some of these issues, or you may not, but they appear often enough that you should be aware of them. These are the issues, arranged from the simplest to the most serious:

1. Confusion about synonymous terms

2. Confusion about ordinary and other income

3. Misconceptions about income

4. Misconceptions about expense

And the two we've already seen:

1. Not understanding the importance of accrual-basis versus cash-basis accounting

2. Not understanding the importance of the matching principle

The first issue, confusion about synonymous terms, is easily cleared up. I used the terms *variable* and *fixed expenses* above to describe the two types of expenses. You will hear other people use different terms to describe the same things. Variable expenses are also called variable costs, cost of goods sold, cost of sales, and direct costs.[15] Some people, including a very vocal accountant I know, will argue that they are somehow different. They aren't. Don't get dragged into that conversation because for our purposes they all mean the same thing. The same is true for fixed expenses. You will hear fixed expenses called fixed costs, overhead expense, indirect costs, administrative

---

15 You may occasionally hear the term "direct costs" applied to overhead expenses that result "directly" from producing a product or service but do not vary from month to month in proportion to sales. For example, a company might separate its recurring monthly payroll into direct payroll (wages paid to people who produce a product or service) and indirect payroll (money paid to administrative staff and salespeople).

INCOME (SALES)

Job income   _____

Product income   _____

Total Income

EXPENSE

Rent   _____

Salaries   _____

Vehicles   _____

Materials   _____

Insurance   _____

Depreciation   _____

Labor   _____

Commissions   _____

Office expense   _____

Total Expense   _____

Net Profit/Loss
(Total Income
minus Total Expense) _____

In the above arrangement, you simply subtract total expenses from total sales to find your net profit or loss. If properly prepared, an income statement arranged like the one above can tell you if you made money, so that's good, and this simple format is all that some businesses need. However, the vast majority of small businesses need an income statement that looks like this one:

Little Co LLC
Profit and Loss
January 1 – December 31, 20xx

Accrual Basis

Income
    Job Income
    Product Income   _____
Total Income Assets

Cost of Goods Sold
    Labor
    Materials
    Commissions   _____
Total Cost of Goods Sold

Gross Profit   _____

Fixed expense
    Rent
    Salaries
    Vehicles
    Depreciations
    Insurance
    Office Expense   _____
Total Expenses   _____

Net Income

The difference between the two reports is that I moved three expense items (labor, materials, and commissions) to a new category called "cost of goods sold (also known as variable expense)." I also added a new line for gross profit. So why the change?

I explained earlier that there are only five types of accounts, one of which is expense. What I didn't say is that there are two kinds of expenses. One is *variable* expense; the other is *fixed* expense. The two should be separated on the income statement because they behave differently in relation to sales and that turns out to be a very important difference.

Variable expenses are expenses that go up and down with sales. For example, if you were to double your sales in a month, variable expenses—in this case, labor, materials, and commissions—would also double.[14] If your sales were cut in half for a month, your variable expenses would also be cut in half.

Fixed expenses, also known as overhead expense, do not go up and down with sales. If you were to double your sales in a month, or to reduce them by half, or if you had no sales at all, your fixed expenses would remain the same. Rent, office salaries, vehicle operating expenses, insurance, and office expenses are fixed expenses in the example above.

Because variable and fixed items are all expenses, both types of income statements show the same income (sales) at the top and the same net profit at the bottom. However, as we will see in chapter 14, it is useful to keep variable and fixed expenses separate on your income statement.

Before moving on, I'm sure some of you are thinking, "All expenses move up and down with sales!" That's true *over a sufficiently long time*. On the one hand, if we don't sell anything over the long haul, our fixed expenses will go down because we will eventually quit paying them. On the other hand, if our sales were to double and keep on doubling, it's a sure bet that our fixed expenses would have to go up to support them (bigger offices, more support staff, higher insurance bills, and so on). So, yes, all expenses are variable over a long period. However, for management purposes, we are concerned with the near term. We want to know how expenses behave *this* month, *this* quarter, and *this* year. In the near term, the two kinds of expenses behave differently and you must keep them separate.

Those are the essentials of an income statement and most of what y need to know about it, at least for now. However, as with many subje that appear simple, the details can trip you up. Years of looking at hundr perhaps thousands, of small business income statements have showr that there are some real land mines in the details. Fortunately, there a

---

14 Variable expenses don't always move up and down *exactly* in proportion to sales rather in a *predictable* proportion to sales. As we will see in Section III, a large part efforts to become more efficient will be finding ways to increase sales in proportio variable costs.

expense, or selling general and administrative (SG&A). Again, they all mean the same thing and refer to expenses that do not go up and down with sales. Regardless of your business and the terms you use, variable expenses go up and down with sales. Fixed expenses don't.

The second issue is two vocabulary terms we haven't discussed but may encounter. The terms are "ordinary" and "other," as in "ordinary or other income" and "ordinary or other expense." I said previously that income is money you receive as a result of selling your products or services and that expenses are money you spend to get the income. The statements are true but they're not the whole story. You can also earn income through unusual activity, such as selling that 40 acres down by the river that's worth a whole lot more than you paid for it 20 years ago. You can also incur expense through unusual activity, such as advertising the sale of the river land. Because neither the income nor the expense from the sale came through normal operations, accountants record them as "other income" and "other expense." They show up at the bottom of the income statement in a section called, not surprisingly, "other income and expense." The section is a mini–income statement that keeps income and expense from *unusual* transactions separate from those from our *normal* business transactions. It's good sense to keep them separate because if they were jumbled together, it would distort the information you need to make decisions about normal operations. We'll use ordinary income and expense for the methods discussed in chapter 14.

The third issue is recognizing what is and is not income. Income is money (or the promise to pay us money) that we receive from selling our products or services. It does not include money we receive from loans or investors or that we contribute to our businesses. Most business owners are pretty clear about that, but I occasionally see loans and owner contributions recorded as income. I recently saw an owner's contribution check included with customer checks in a deposit recorded as sales. Including loans or contributions in income not only distorts profit but also results in a higher tax bill (as we saw happen to the furniture dealer back in chapter 1).

The fourth issue is confusion about what is and is not an expense. I come across confusion surrounding expenses much more often than with income. People seem naturally inclined to treat any expenditure as an expense. However, just because you wrote a check for a purchase (or because you bought something on credit) does not mean the purchase was an expense. I often see vehicle, mortgage, credit card, and bank loan payments listed as expenses on income statements. These items are not expenses.

Interest on the debt is an expense, and what you bought with the loans or credit cards *might* have been expenses, but *repayment of debt is not an expense.* That idea confuses a lot of people. If you're one of them, think about it this way: When you use borrowed money to pay an expense, you recorded the expense in your books. If you later record repayment of the debt as an expense, you will have recorded the expense twice. I also come across owner's distributions (draws), income tax payments,[16] and the cost of purchased assets recorded as expenses. Those are not expenses, either, and they do not belong on the income statement. It's confusing and tedious to separate payments into interest and principal, to determine what taxes are expenses and what items are assets, and to get it all recorded properly in your books. You can spend your time trying to learn how to do all that or you can hire competent professionals to keep your books or at least review and adjust them.

The fifth issue is cash-basis versus accrual-basis reports. We've seen how cash-basis books can distort an income statement. For example, if you were to make a $100,000 sale and allow your customer 30 days to pay, the sale would not appear on your current income statement and would result in understated profit. If you were to purchase $50,000 worth of supplies on credit, the expense would not appear on the current report, which would result in overstated profits. At any given time, missing transactions on cash-basis books include both sales and expenses. That makes it difficult to know if profits are overstated or understated, which renders your income statement almost useless.

Because it's far more accurate and complete than the cash-basis method,

---

16 In some forms of corporations, taxes are an expense that can be charged to the business, but this is not true of most small business entities.

you must keep your books and prepare all your reports using the accrual method. As I said earlier, don't worry if your accountant tells you that you pay taxes on the cash basis. Accountants can easily create cash-basis tax returns from accrual-based books. They cannot create accrual-basis reports from cash-basis books.

The last issue, matching, is the really tough one. Matching sales in a given period with expenses incurred in the same period can be difficult but it's a really big deal to get it right. In businesses such as service providers, it's not too difficult to match sales and expenses. That's because the sales and the cost of the sales happen at the same time and place. In other businesses, as we saw with the example companies above, it's not so easy.

You don't have to be a contractor or manufacturer to have matching issues. Let's say your liability insurance for the next 12 months is $48,000, which includes a discount as an incentive to pay the whole amount in January. Recording a $48,000 expense in January would be a big hit that would distort the month's income statement. For that reason, you should match the expense on your books by spreading the cost over the year at $4,000 per month.[17]

Confusion around matching usually smooths out after the end of the year. That's because in order to pay taxes, you set a stopping point at year-end, count your inventory, wait for payments and bills to roll in, and record it all in last year's books. You give your accountant your books and inventory counts and let them figure out the numbers. Then typically, months after year-end, you can say with some confidence whether or not you made a profit *for the prior year*. Accountants routinely correct matching and other mistakes in order to prepare your tax return but that's not good enough. Their corrections keep you out of trouble with the IRS but you have to have accurate financial statements as you work through the year. You cannot afford to wait until sometime next year to see if you made a profit last month.

Problems with the first five issues are relatively easy to fix but matching

---

17 You may not know how to do that but your accountant does.

can be tough. Unfortunately, *matching is not optional*. Your bookkeeper and accountant must do it or your books and reports will be useless for management purposes.

We haven't spent time explaining how to keep proper accrual-basis books or how to prepare an accurate income statement and we're not going to in this book. It's your accountant's or bookkeeper's role to understand *how* it's done and to do it. It's your role to see to it *that it's done*.

Important things to know about the income statement:

1. It answers the question "Are we making money?"

2. It's a period statement that shows income and expense incurred between two dates.

3. It must be reported on the accrual basis.

4. It must be arranged to keep variable and fixed costs separate and to show gross profit.

5. Income must be matched with incurred expenses. It is not sufficient to correct the statement at year-end.

6. You should have a professional bookkeeper or CPA who is concerned with management as well as taxes. They should review your books at least monthly to ensure the income statements you rely on are timely, accurate, and useful.

The next standard statement is the balance sheet which answers the questions: What do we own? What do we owe? What's left over?

CHAPTER 11

The Balance Sheet: "What Do We Own? What Do We Owe? What's Left Over?"

If business were medicine, the income statement would report our choices between donuts and broccoli since our last visit to our cardiologist. The balance sheet would report the results of today's exam.

—Unknown

T HE BALANCE SHEET IS LESS INTUITIVE THAN THE INCOME STATEMENT BUT it's not hard to understand. The report is essentially a list of what you own, what you owe, and the difference between the two, which is your net worth.

You have probably produced at least the occasional balance sheet, if for no other reason than because a bank asked you to fill out an application for a loan. The application form instructs you to list what you own and what you owe and then to subtract the latter from the former to estimate your net worth. You probably dreaded the task because it's a tedious exercise to recall everything and to assign each item a value. You may be especially apprehensive because you have to sign your name attesting to the accuracy of what you listed. (If you had proper books, all you would have to do is click PRINT instead of working from memory.)

Unlike the income statement, which shows what happened *between two dates*, the balance sheet is often described as a "snapshot report" that shows the condition of a business *as of a specific date.*[18] The balance sheet is a more strategic report than the income statement. That's why most small business owners spend a lot more time with their income statements than they do with their balance sheets.

Through an ingenious process, the balance sheet combines information from your income statement (income and expense accounts) with information from asset, liability, and equity accounts to provide a picture of the condition of your company. It's a fascinating report that shows the *cumulative effect of every transaction in the history of your business* from inception through the day (and moment!) of the report. Changes in net worth over time reflect the ultimate score that tells you how well you've run your company in the past.

Robert Bauman owns a cabinet manufacturing company that has grown steadily over the last few years. We will meet him again in chapter 14 when we see how he used numbers to solve a perplexing problem. He was (and still is) the best in his company at everything from sales to part cutting, from troubleshooting to handling customer complaints—everything. He could do it all and he did. He devoted his time and attention to working in the business and handling problems as they arose, but he knew that if things didn't change, the potential of his company would forever be limited to his personal capacity to get things done. As his business grew, it became apparent that he couldn't perform all four business functions by himself. He decided to hand off production duties as his first foray into serious delegation. He reasoned that freeing himself from production duties would free up more of his time than delegating other tasks.

---

18 QuickBooks will ask you to enter "from" and "to" dates for the balance sheet report. They do that for reasons unknown to me, but don't let the fact that they ask for two dates confuse you. The date that matters is the "to," or ending, date, which will produce a report *as of* that date.

Robert began his search for a chief operating officer to take over plant operations. Through networking and luck, he met a highly experienced production engineer who had just become available in his area. The engineer spent 30 years managing different production facilities for a huge, publicly traded German company. To say the engineer was sophisticated is an understatement. The German company was shutting down a local facility and wanted the engineer to relocate. He didn't want to move and was looking for other opportunities. Robert's company seemed to fit the bill. What a stroke of good fortune!

As Robert showed the engineer around his facility, their conversation highlighted the differences between how large and small companies approach production and measure results. They discussed subjects such as Six Sigma,[19] lean manufacturing, inventory management, and other production topics, but what struck Robert the most was the engineer's grasp of financial reports. Although he was a production man, he was intimately familiar with financial reports. The German company managed by the numbers, and the engineer's performance evaluations and compensation were directly tied to financial reports.

As they wrapped up a three-hour conversation, the engineer's final words to Robert were, "It's apparent that you still manage by the income statement. There will come a time when you transition to managing by the balance sheet."

Robert called me immediately after their conversation and asked, "What did he mean by that?"

Consistent with the beliefs and types of thinking we saw in chapter 7, the engineer was saying in his own way that Robert managed his company as a *calloused owner* rather than a *master investor*. The distinction is that a calloused owner manages for profit and cash. A master investor manages to increase the value of the company, which is the realm of the balance sheet and the subject of chapter 19.

---

19 Six Sigma is a data-driven approach to constantly improving systems and eliminating defects in products.

The Balance Sheet

The balance sheet has two broad applications. The first application is as a list of important facts about the business. The second and less obvious use is as a tool to diagnose the financial health of the company and to do strategic planning. Most business owners do not use their balance sheets at all, but if they do, they use them as lists of useful information. To illustrate my point, answer quickly: How much cash do you have available right now? Not "about" how much, *exactly* how much? Exactly how much do you owe on your truck and your real estate mortgage? Exactly how much do your customers owe you, and how much do you owe your suppliers? Exactly how much money have you taken out of your company as draws (this month, this year, and total)? There is a better-than-even chance you don't know, but if you do, it's because you have a good balance sheet.

Those are important questions, yet very few small business owners can answer them. You might estimate your cash by looking at an online banking app but that doesn't show the effects of outstanding checks or deposits. (You still write a few checks, right?) You may have a pretty good idea of what you owe on your truck or real estate loan but you probably don't know *exactly* how much. If you're like most business owners I've met, you also don't know how much money you've taken out of your business as draws.

There are important reasons beyond peace of mind to know the answers to all those questions. You need to know how much cash you have available, if for no other reason than to be sure you don't write checks on a negative bank balance. You need to know how much you owe on debt in order to judge the health of your company or to approach a bank for a loan. You should know how much money you are taking out of the company. As we will see later in our discussion of the statement of cash flows, owner draws are often a significant source of cash flow problems. If you have a current balance sheet, you have all that information—and more—available to you at the click of a mouse.

The underlying idea behind the balance sheet is that *everything* a business owns—its assets—is owed to *someone*. If the obligation is to a nonowner, such as a bank or a supplier, it's called a *liability*. If the obligation is to an owner, it's called *equity*. Because the business owes *everything* to *someone*, total assets must always equal the combined total of liabilities plus equity; in other words, the two totals must "balance."

When you subtract liabilities from assets, the remainder is owners' equity, or "net worth." Net worth comes after liabilities both on the balance sheet and in terms of priority because *owners get paid last*. That's right. We may own the companies but as owners, we get paid last. If you don't believe that, try paying yourself while leaving the government, your vendors, lenders, and employees unpaid. People will come looking for you and when they find you, you'll lose. They will get their money. (Welcome to the world of business ownership!) Compensating yourself for that risk is among the reasons you should take draws or distributions from your company *in addition to the paycheck* you earn as compensation for the work you do.

Balance sheets are arranged in a conventional order. Asset accounts are listed first, liability accounts second, and equity accounts last. Within each group, accounts are listed in order of *liquidity*, which is an indication of how fast the account might provide or consume cash.[20] Short-term assets are those that can be quickly converted to cash. For example, the account "cash in the bank" is something we own and it *is* cash. It's listed as the first asset because available cash is the first thing *everybody* wants to know. The next item is usually accounts receivable based on the presumption that accounts receivable are due soon and that people will pay us quickly. (They will pay us quickly, right?) Inventory usually comes next, again based on the presumption that inventory can be sold and converted to cash quickly. These short-term assets are followed by long-term assets such as equipment and trucks and finally by assets such as buildings and land, most of which would take a considerable amount of time to convert to cash.

The asset portion of our balance sheet might look like this:

---

20 You may not use the term "liquidity" but you are familiar with the concept. Liquid assets are the assets you first think about when you are scrambling to come up with cash. Short-term *liabilities* are likely to be the reason you are scrambling for cash in the first place.

ASSETS
Short-Term Assets
    Cash in bank
    Accounts receivable
    Inventory
Long-Term Assets
    Trucks
    Equipment
    Building and land
    Accumulated depreciation

Total Assets

After assets come liabilities, also grouped as short-term and long-term and arranged in the order of liquidity. Accounts payable is usually listed first among liabilities because suppliers expect to be paid soon, usually within 30 days, and cash is required to pay them. After accounts payable come credit cards and short-term loans due over the next few years, such as a loan for a truck. Last are longer-term debts, such as mortgages for land and buildings, that are due more than a few years out.

The liabilities portion of our balance sheet might look like this:

LIABILITIES
Short-Term Liabilities
    Accounts payable
    Credit cards
Long-Term Liabilities
    Loan on truck
    Bank loan, land, and building

Total Liabilities

The final group of accounts is made up of the equity accounts. These are arranged in a standard order, not in order of liquidity. In some types of business structures, tax rules dictate how to keep track of equity accounts (which is another reason to work with a good accountant), but even then, the order is pretty much standard.

Paid-in capital is first among equity accounts. Paid-in capital is the original amount you paid into a business banking account to start the company way back when. Paid-in capital is followed by a contributions account that keeps track of additional money you (and other owners) paid into the company. Next is a withdrawal account that shows how much you and the other owners have taken out of the business as draws or dividends.[21] You might see the contributions and withdrawal accounts combined into one account that shows the net difference between what was paid in and taken out, with all the pluses and minuses added up to give a single "balance." The contributions account balance can be positive or negative, depending on whether you have put more money into the company as contributions than you've taken out as draws.

The last two equity accounts are cumulative earnings and current earnings. The cumulative earnings total is a fascinating number. It shows the cumulative total of net profits or losses from the *day the business began* through the last day of the *last* business year.

The current earnings line shows how much money the business has made or lost so far *this year*. If you add cumulative earnings and current earnings together, you can see how much the company has earned from the day it began to the day of the report.

When you're looking at a set of financial reports for the same period, the current earnings number on the balance sheet should be *exactly* the same as the net profit number on the income statement. If it isn't, something is wrong.

---

21 Your salary as an owner is not listed here. Your salary is an expense that should be listed on your income statement.

The equity portion of our balance sheet might look like this:

Equity
  Paid-in capital
  Owner contributions
  Owner withdrawals
  Cumulative earnings
  Current earnings
Total Equity

Total equity is the sum of all the numbers listed above it in the equity section of the balance sheet. Total equity is a very important number for two reasons. First, it enables tax professionals to work calculations that affect taxes and rules governing distributions among owners. Second, it shows the amount that would be left over for the owners if all assets were sold and all liabilities paid at the recorded amounts. We will expand on this idea of so-called book value later.

Putting all three groups of account types together without any details, we get a balance sheet that looks like the one below. We know that our balance sheet "balances" when total assets equal the sum of liabilities plus equity. It's not hard to get a balance sheet to balance when using computer programs such as QuickBooks.

ASSETS
Short-Term Assets
Cash in bank

Accounts receivable

Inventory
Total Short-Term Assets

Long-Term Assets
Trucks

Equipment

Building and land

Accumulated depreciation
Net Long-Term Assets
TOTAL ASSETS

LIABILITIES
Short-Term Liabilities
Accounts payable

Credit cards
Total Current Liabilities

Long-Term Liabilities
Loan on truck

Mortgage: land and building

Operating loan
Total Long-Term Liabilities
Total Liabilities

EQUITY
Paid-in capital

Owner contributions

Owner withdrawals

Cumulative earnings

Current earnings
Total Equity
TOTAL LIABILITY PLUS EQUITY

Total Liabilities Plus Equity

Total Liabilities plus Equity is the sum of Total liabilities plus Total Equity and should exactly equal Total Assets. It's not likely that your balance sheet will be as simple as the one above. There will be more accounts, some of which you won't recognize at first. However, as long as you understand that assets are things the business owns, liabilities are things the business owes, and equity is what's left over for the owners, you should be able to understand what you're looking at.

We've just described the basic elements of the balance sheet and its use as a list of information and already you can use it to find:

1. How much cash you have available

2. How much your customers owe you (your accounts receivable)

3. What you own (your total assets)

4. How much you've spent on long-term assets

5. How much of the value of your long-term assets you've written off (accumulated depreciation)

6. What you owe your suppliers (your accounts payable)

7. Your total debt (total liabilities)

8. The net worth of the business (The balance sheet shows you the calculated net value of the business. As we will see, your business could be worth much more or less than what shows on your balance sheet.)

9. How much money you've put into the business since inception (the sum of paid-in capital and owner contributions)

10. How much money you've taken out of the business since inception (your withdrawals)

11. How much money the business has earned since it began (your retained earnings)

12. How much money it has earned so far this year (your current earnings)

13. How much and how quickly you are likely to convert assets into cash (your short-term assets)

14. How much and how quickly you will need cash to meet your debt payments (your short-term liabilities)

15. How much you owe on your credit cards

16. How much you owe on vehicle and bank loans

That's a whole lot of useful information. All of us have tried keeping track of it in our heads. Consider the days you spent driving around trying to do mental math: Who might pay me this week? How much do I owe suppliers? Who is due now, and who is due a little later? Can I hold them off long enough to order materials for this job before they put me on credit hold? Are receivables enough to cover all the payables? I wonder how much I owe on the payroll tax deposit and, damn, I forgot about the mortgage payment due this week, and so on and so on. At best, the mental exercise is a worrisome distraction that keeps you from your work, and at worst, it leads to bad decisions. It's impossible to keep track of it all in your head, but with good books, the information is available on the balance sheet at the click of a button. You can know—you don't have to guess.

Those are the basics of using the balance sheet as a list of information, but before we move on to the statement of cash flows, we need to talk about the concept of "book value." Book value, as we saw above, is the value of assets, liabilities, and net worth *as they appear in your books and on your financial reports.* The thing to know about book value is that it's almost certainly inaccurate. It may not be even close to the *actual* value of your assets and company for two principle reasons. The first is market value and the second is depreciation.

Market value is what something is worth at a given time and place. Market values are constantly changing, and for that reason, the true value of your assets and company are constantly changing. You just don't know with certainty whether the value is going up or down, or by how much.

That much should be clear, but you also know (boy, do you know!) that your inventory may no longer be worth what you paid for it due to damage or obsolescence. You also know that you may not be able to collect all the receivables listed on your balance sheet. Accounting rules make allowances to reduce the recorded value of assets that are clearly worth less or worthless. Occasionally, with a proper appraisal, an accountant can change the recorded value of real estate assets to reflect an appraised market value. But for the most part, your balance sheet records the condition of your company based on amounts resulting from past transactions. Assets are valued at cost—the price you paid for them or the price someone has agreed to pay you. Liabilities are valued at the amount you agreed to pay. The differences between actual market value and the prices you paid or agreed to pay mean that the book value of your assets and company is almost certainly inaccurate. You just can't know with certainty by how much or in which direction the values are off.

The second reason your balance sheet is inaccurate is depreciation. You've likely heard of it. The word appeared on our sample income statement as an expense named "depreciation." We'll see it again on the Statement of Cash Flows. Depreciation is an expense but it's a special kind of expense. It's different because you don't actually *pay* depreciation as you do a utility bill or rent. It's a "noncash" expense that reduces our profit like any other expense, but it's simply a bookkeeping entry that doesn't require us to pay out any cash. Second, depreciation is not an asset, liability, or equity account, yet it appears as "accumulated depreciation" on your balance sheet.[22]

Recall from the definition of cost above that we spend money on both expense items and assets. We said that an expense item, such as gasoline, is

---

22 Technically speaking, depreciation is an expense, and accumulated depreciation is a special "contra-asset" account. We don't need to worry about that distinction but aren't you glad we cleared it up?

entirely used up in the current accounting period. An asset, such as the truck that burned the gas, is not *entirely* used up—but *some* of it is. Long-term assets, such as trucks, equipment, and buildings that wear out over a long time are called *depreciable assets*. Depreciation expense is supposed to be an estimate of how much they wore out and, consequently, how much their value declined in an accounting period. I said "supposed to be" because that's not really how it works.

Depreciation, like any other expense, reduces taxable profit. On the one hand, we business owners generally *dislike* taxes and want to expense, or "write off," as much as possible. On the other hand, governments *like* taxes and prefer we not do that. Those conflicting interests have resulted in complex and constantly changing rules about how quickly we may write off depreciable assets. Therefore, depreciation expenses are determined more by tax rules than by the actual wear and tear on the assets or by their actual decline in value. Depending on the rules in force at the time, some assets are written off faster and some slower than their actual decrease in value. For that reason, the value of depreciable assets shown on our balance sheets is almost certainly inaccurate.

Accountants use accumulated depreciation on the balance sheet to preserve and show detail. The detail helps compensate for the distorted picture resulting from depreciation. To understand how it works, assume that over the life of your business you purchased a total of $20 million worth of machinery and equipment assets, all of which you duly recorded on your balance sheet. Let's also assume that the government has allowed you to write off $20 million of depreciation expense against those assets over the same period. If you were to simply net out those two numbers, you would see a big fat zero next to "long-term assets" on your balance sheet. There would be no evidence remaining to show you had ever purchased them.

Now suppose a bank or an investor was comparing your balance sheet to that of a young company that had purchased, but not yet depreciated, $1 million in assets. The young company would show $1 million in long-term assets on its balance sheet. It would appear, at least on paper, to be more substantial than your company, which shows zero long-term assets on the balance sheet, even though you still own and operate assets that cost $20 million. To preserve the distinction, accountants show both the value of the assets at the time they were purchased and the accumulated depreciation charged against them on the balance sheet

If the value of your assets is inaccurate because of changing market values and depreciation, then the book value of your net worth, which depends on assets, is also inaccurate. So why not just change the values in our books? Why not just double the value of that stale inventory you couldn't sell that's been sitting on the bottom of the pallet pile for five years, and report *that* to your banker? Because there has to be some generally accepted standard governing the book values so people can understand what they're looking at. That standard is cost.

You show assets on your books at cost because guesses or estimates are not reliably accurate, consistent, or generally accepted gauges of value. The numbers in proper books come from *cost* validated by actual transactions, preferably among unrelated people or entities, which are known as "arm's-length transactions." Such transactions represent opinion but they are opinion backed by money.

Thus far, we've talked about the balance sheet as if it were merely a list of useful information but it's much more than that. In chapter 15, we'll see how the balance sheet provides both useful insights into the health of a company and information we need to make strategic decisions about the future. You will get the most strategic insights and information from your balance sheet through ratios that are expressed as "something per something." I think you will be startled to learn the depth of understanding available through the apparently benign and simple balance sheet.

Just three more comments on the balance sheet and then we'll move on to the statement of cash flows. First, if you have been running your business without proper books and are ready to do things right, the transformation begins with an accurate balance sheet (and an accountant's help). To begin, you must create a list of what you own and what you owe through a process similar to filling out a loan application. Your accountant will want access to your bank and credit card accounts. They will want to see your equipment loans, leases, mortgages, depreciation schedules, and more. Your accountant will use that information along with your prior years' tax returns to create a solid foundation for your books going forward. It will be a tedious and difficult process (if it's not, then your accountant is probably not doing a good job) but take heart. The results will be worth the effort. The payoff is the peace of mind that comes from knowing rather than guessing and from access to information you need to make better decisions and more money.

Second, hire an accountant to review and close your books every month. Closing your books is a process of reconciling every account on the balance sheet (not just your bank accounts). Closing is critical for accuracy, giving you a baseline to go back to when things don't balance and providing your first line of defense against embezzlement, as we will see in chapter 20.

Third, the balance sheet provides most of the information used in the statement of cash flows. It would be impossible to create a statement of cash flows, a very important and useful report, without an accurate balance sheet.

That's an overview of the balance sheet. The important things to know about it are:

1. A balance sheet answers the questions: "What do I own? What do I owe? And what's left over for me?" (We will see in chapters 12 and 16 that it answers many more questions.)

2. It's a snapshot report that shows the net effects of every transaction in the history of the company as of a specific date.

3. It must be prepared on the accrual basis.

4. The standard order of accounts on a balance sheet is assets, liabilities, and equity.

5. Asset and liability accounts are listed in order of liquidity, with items likely to provide or use cash listed first in each account type.

6. The amounts shown on the balance sheet are based on arm's-length

transactions and, due to changing market values and depreciation, are almost certainly inaccurate.

7. You should have a professional, one who is concerned with management as well as taxes, reconcile every balance sheet account each month.

8. The balance sheet contains a list of useful information, which can be used to diagnose the condition of your business.

Let's move on to the tremendously important statement of cash flows, which answers this question: Where did our cash go?

CHAPTER 12

The Statement of Cash Flows: "Where Did Our Cash Go?"

We imagined ourselves smoking fat cigars
And paying off debt and driving new cars,
But our dreams had to wait for another day,
Because we couldn't spend a promise to pay.

—From "A Promise to Pay"

I REMEMBER MEETING WITH ROGER, THE OWNER AND CEO OF AN $80 MIL-lion (sales) company.[23] He and I sat in a restaurant booth having lunch, and he talked in level tones about the issues at work, most of which had to do with employee performance and market conditions. Imagine my surprise when, midway through our conversation, his tone and expression darkened abruptly and he pounded the table with his fist.

"Damn it!" he said too loudly for the surroundings. "They say I make money, so why don't I have any?"

---

23 It's always fun talking with Roger. Before changing the subject from people to cash, he had blurted out, "All I want in an employee is someone who will exceed my expectations!" He must have noticed the expression on my face because he quickly added, "And that doesn't take much!"

It was immediately apparent what was really on his mind. Although I didn't expect to hear that question from the owner of an $80 million company with a full-time CFO, I wasn't really surprised because I hear the question almost every week. Answer the question and manage accordingly and an insufferable burden of stress will lift from your shoulders.

I responded, "Let's look at your statement of cash flows, and I'll show you exactly why you don't have any money."

He narrowed his eyes. "My what?"

After repeating my request, it was obvious to me he had never heard of a statement of cash flows.

Despite the importance of cash and our preoccupation with it, I don't recall ever meeting a small business owner who had even *heard* of the statement of cash flows, let alone seen or understood it. Based on my experience explaining the report to small business owners, it's not at all intuitive, at least not at first.

If you're suffering from cash flow problems, and I'll bet that you are, history suggests that you aren't alone. Cash flow problems date back to Pacioli and beyond, but the statement of cash flows is new, or at least relatively new. It wasn't until the early 1970s that the report officially joined the income statement and balance sheet as the third of three standard financial statements.

You don't have to understand bookkeeping or financial statements to understand the importance of cash. Creditors will explain it to you and if they don't, the IRS will. Everybody wants your cash: Payroll this week, suppliers next week, debt service the week after, and tax deposits, seemingly, all the time. Even when you make a profit, it feels as if you're in a perpetual scramble for scarce cash.

The Spanish name for cash describes it perfectly—*dinero efectivo.* "Effective money," as opposed to "ineffective" money such as that tied up in accounts receivable or inventory. I heard a hedge fund manager say that if profit and sales were food and water, then cash would be oxygen. That's because a business can survive indefinitely without profit or sales but no company can make it past Friday's payroll without cash.

The Statement of Cash Flows

Like the income statement, the statement of cash flows is a period statement. It uses information from your income statement and balance sheet to tell you where your cash came from and where it went *between two specific dates*. Once you're familiar with the report and what it tells you, you'll see that it makes perfect sense and will find it to be immensely useful. It highlights your exact cash flow. The benefit of that knowledge is that once you identify a problem, you can do something about it.

Before we look at the report itself, let's look at the logic behind it. The report does simple arithmetic by adding and subtracting a list of numbers to get a final total. The first number is your cash balance at the beginning of the reporting period, which makes perfect sense.[24] That's the starting point. The next number is the profit (or loss) you made in the period, and that number is followed by a list of positive and negative numbers resulting from activities that either provided (positive numbers) or used (negative numbers) cash. The final number is the sum of all the positive and negative numbers and equals your ending cash balance as of the date of the report. Once again, if you're looking at all three financial reports prepared for the same period, the ending cash balance on your statement of cash flows should be exactly the same as the cash balance shown on your balance sheet.

To begin, let's revisit our original question: "They say I make money, so why don't I have any?" Implied in the question is this assumption: "Profit means my income was more than my expense. So if I made a profit, I *should* have more cash than I started with." That is a logical, well-reasoned assumption but as we will see, it's wrong. If you're making money but don't have any, there are three possible reasons:

---

24 Unfortunately, some bookkeeping programs put the beginning balance number toward the bottom of the report. Regardless of where it's located on the report, it's the starting point.

1. Your customers haven't paid you yet.

2. You already spent the money paying off debt or buying assets.

3. You, the owner, took it.

The first reason is that your customers haven't paid you yet. Sales are the source of profit but making a sale doesn't mean you were paid. Customers who buy on credit contribute to profit but don't contribute to cash. In the language of cash flow, accounts receivable are said to "use" or "consume" cash. The part of your profit that came from credit sales is not available as cash. We all know that but we don't always *realize* it. This was the lesson the business owner in chapter 7 learned the hard way. He made a very nice profit on burgeoning sales but his business was close to death from cash asphyxiation.

The second reason is that you already spent the money. Even if you made a profit, and even if all of your customers paid you, you still wouldn't have any cash if you spent it repaying debt or buying assets. Recall that money spent repaying debt is not an expense and does not reduce profit. Money spent buying assets, such as inventory, vehicles, equipment, or real estate is not an expense because expenses, by definition, are "written off" in the current accounting period. Assets, by definition, are not. If you made a profit but don't have any cash, it could be because you generated enough profit to pay all your expenses but not enough to also buy assets and repay debt.

The third reason is that you took the money. There's nothing wrong with taking cash from your company. After all, that's the point, but when it comes to accounting for cash, the *salary you take is an expense* that reduces profit. The *cash you take as draws is not an expense* and does not reduce profit. Instead, draws are a distribution *of* profit. For a majority of us, the same is true of income taxes. For most small business entities, *income taxes are not expenses* and do not affect profit. They are the government's share of profits. Whether or not you realize it, when you pay your taxes, you first take the money out of your company as a draw and then pass it along to the government. That means, from the bookkeeping point of view, that taxes are just a form of distributions.[25]

How much do you take from your business?

Allison is an example of an owner whose draws dramatically affected her cash on hand. She had no idea. Allison built her commercial cleaning company from scratch to more than $1 million in sales in just a few years. She also keeps good and proper books.

"So how is it," she asked me after reviewing her income statement, "that I make money but never seem to have any?"

We ran through a series of questions: "Do you have a lot of accounts receivable?" Hardly any. "Are you paying down debt?" She didn't have any debt except a couple of small car payments. "Have you bought a lot of assets?" Again, no.

"Well," I said, "you must be taking the money out as draws."

Allison assured me that wasn't the case.

"So how much money *did* you take out of the company over the last three months?" I asked.

"Not much. There would have been our personal car payments, and I use the company debit card for a few things when I'm out shopping. So maybe $1,500?" she guessed.

"Let's look," I said.

I clicked on her statement of cash flows report in QuickBooks and there was the answer. It showed she had drawn out a little more than $18,000 over the last three months.

---

25 That may not be the way you think of it but that is the way the government requires you to treat most tax payments. Taxes for most small businesses are treated as distributions of profit. They are not expenses and you cannot write them off on your income statements.

"That's not possible!" she protested. We clicked down in the report to see details, and sure enough, there were itemized charges. My guess was that her draws averaged less than $100 each but she had made a lot of them. She was absolutely flabbergasted but to her credit, she put herself on a strict budget and reduced her draws to $5,000 per quarter. Problem solved.

Allison's story may surprise you. How could anyone not know they had withdrawn $18,000 in a few months? If you're surprised, test yourself. How much did you take out of your business last quarter? Write down your guess and then go find the real number. Congratulations if your guess is within 25 percent of the real number!

We've seen how it's possible to make a boatload of money but run out of cash by spending two boatloads of money on things that don't directly affect profit. *Understanding* why we run out of cash may be difficult but running out of cash is easy to do based on how many of us do it.

There are two cautionary lessons to take away from this discussion so far. The first is that profit is only a part of our cash picture. The second is that the income statement by itself is not a good indicator of our cash position. There is a third and less obvious lesson, one you won't hear much about because people seldom complain about an abundance of cash.

More cash than profit

On happy occasions, we may find ourselves wondering why we produce more cash than profit. Maybe we haven't seen our income statement for a while but our online banking app shows that we have a surprising amount of cash on hand. That's a pleasant, albeit dangerous, position to be in. Pleasant—because who doesn't love a cash surplus? Dangerous—because if you don't understand how it happened, you are likely to misspend it.

How can it happen? The first reason is that the three explanations for cash shortages also work in reverse. The second reason is that depreciation is a noncash expense that reduces profit but not cash. You may find yourself with an unexpected abundance of cash for one or more of the following reasons:

1. You collected more than you sold.

2. You borrowed more than you repaid.

3. You sold more assets than you bought.

4. You put more money into the business than you took out.

5. You have a lot of depreciation expense.

The first explanation is that your collections for the period were more than your sales. Sometimes you collect more cash from past accounts receivable than you tie up in new accounts receivable. This is what happened to Carolyn and Rodney, the contractor and his wife. Their operating losses were obscured by cash coming in from sales made the prior year. You might also accumulate an abundance of cash if you're among the enlightened few, such as Michael, the calloused business owner, who collects deposits in advance of future sales. In either case, your cash collections could exceed the profit shown on your income statements.

The second explanation could be that you brought in more cash than you spent on non-expense items. That might be because you borrowed more from your suppliers, credit cards, or banks than you repaid. You might also have increased your cash by selling more inventory than you bought in a period or by selling assets such as trucks, equipment, or real estate. Depending on accounting rules, selling assets can increase cash without increasing income.

The third explanation is pretty straightforward: you put more cash into the company than you took out as distributions.

The fourth and last explanation involves the special matter of depreciation. Depreciation reduces profit because it's an expense but it doesn't consume cash because you don't actually "pay" for depreciation. It's simply a bookkeeping entry. In accounting terms, depreciation expense is said to "provide" cash. That makes sense because it adds back the expense that reduced your profit on the income statement. Some businesses manage depreciation so well that they generate surplus cash, even when they show losses on their income statements.

The danger of having an unexpectedly high cash balance is a natural inclination to spend the money on things you don't need or can't afford. Like Rodney, when you find yourself flush with an unexpectedly high cash balance, it's easy to convince yourself to buy equipment, pay down your mortgage, or take a draw to fund a vacation, only to regret the decision when the payables and credit cards come due. When you have an unexpectedly high cash balance, you have to know why and act accordingly.

In the real world of business, your cash balance is the result of hundreds or thousands of decisions and transactions. Some provide cash and others consume it—and the net result changes constantly. You cannot keep track of it in your head. How in the world can you understand, let alone manage, the ebb and flow of cash in that environment? You can't do it by guessing and it's far too important to leave to chance. Managing cash requires information, understanding, and decision-making. Managing cash requires the statement of cash flows.

The statement explained

As you look at a statement of cash flows, keep in mind what's going on. It begins with the cash you have and adds or subtracts profit (or loss) and a list of other factors that affect cash. The *sum of all those positive and negative numbers is your ending cash balance*. It's that simple but it will not *seem* simple at first.

Your statement of cash flows will look a lot like the one below. Yours may be arranged a little differently depending on what software produced it but all the same elements will be there. Do not stress if it isn't immediately clear. *Nobody* gets it at first, and besides, I'll give you a shortcut that will enable you to use the report even if you don't fully understand it.

The report lists your beginning cash balance first. That's the amount of cash you had on hand on the first day of the reporting period. So far, so good, but things can get confusing after that. The beginning cash balance is followed by items grouped into three categories:[26]

1. Changes in cash due to operations

2. Changes in cash due to investments

3. Changes in cash due to financing

The changes due to operations section begins with the profit or loss for the period and then lists the changes in cash that result from normal operating activities. Changes due to operations include activities that directly affect current assets, such as cash in the bank, accounts receivable, and inventory, as well as current liabilities such as accounts payable and credit card debt. There are countless possible combinations of those factors. Some consume and some provide cash, but the report adds all the changes to produce a single number. That number, positive or negative, is shown on the report as "net change due to operations."

The "changes due to investments" section shows how much cash was consumed or provided by buying or selling long-term assets, such as trucks, equipment, or real estate. Buying a long-term asset, an "investment," consumes cash. Selling a long-term asset provides cash. The sum of the positive and negative cash changes from buying or selling assets and also totals a single number shown on the report as "net change due to investments."

The "changes due to financing" section shows how much cash the company either brought in from loans and contributions or paid out to lenders and owners. Once again, the sum of the positive and negative changes in loans and contributions totals a single number shown on the report as "net change due to financing."

---

26 Although the statement of cash flows groups line items into different categories, every line on the report falls under one of the three reasons your cash is different from your profit: you haven't been paid yet, you already spent the cash buying assets or repaying debt, or you took the cash as draws.

The report totals those three sections (cash from operations, investing, and financing) to show a "net changes to cash" for the period. It adds that number to your beginning cash balance to give you your current cash balance. Simple, right? Okay, maybe it's not so simple and that's why so few of us use the statement of cash flows. But one thing is for sure: Once you fully understand the statement, you will find it to be invaluable. You'll wonder how you ever survived without it.

Your statement of cash flows report will look something like this but with numbers, of course:

Little Co LLC
Statement of Cash Flows
January - December 20xx

	Total
Beginning Cash Balance	_____
Changes Due to Operations	
Net Profit for the Period	
Accounts Receivable (A/R)	
Accounts Payable (A/P)	
Inventory	
Credit Cards	
Depreciation	_____
Net Cash Provided by Operating Activities	
Changes Due to Investing Activities	
Truck: F250 Diesel Original Cost	_____
Net Cash Provided by Investing Activities	
Changes Due to Financing Activities	
Notes on F250 Diesel	
Changes to Operating Note	
Changes to Real Estate Mortgage	
Owner's Net Withdrawals and Contributions	_____
Net Cash Provided by Financing Activities	
Net Cash Increase/Decrease for the Period	
Cash at the End of Period	_____

The first thing to know about the report is that any of the numbers can be positive or negative. A negative number next to an item means the item consumed cash. A positive number means the item provided cash. This is what you need to know even if you don't understand the report itself.

The second thing to know is that the numbers on the report (apart from beginning and ending cash) are *changes*, not balances. For example, the number next to accounts receivable is *not* the total of your accounts receivable. It's how much accounts receivable went up or down over the period. Understanding that the numbers are changes, not balances, *is the first major sticking point* for people laboring to understand the statement of cash flows. We will discuss this further in chapter 16.

That brings us to a third inevitable sticking point. In the case of accounts receivable, a *negative* number on the statement of cash flows report means that accounts receivable went *up* by that amount. A positive number means accounts receivables went *down* by that amount. (I warned you the statement of cash flows is confusing. If you're frustrated, just skip ahead to the "Shortcut" section.)

"*Are you kidding me?*" you're thinking. "Down means up, and up means down?" Yes, in the case of accounts receivable, it does. Think about a $10,000 sale you made to a customer, you know, the one who promised to pay you in 30 days "or so." The sale counted as income, but in effect, *you lent him the $10,000* to buy your product. Lending money to customers consumes cash so your cash goes down when accounts receivable go up and your cash goes up when receivables go down. You have less cash available when you lend more of it to your customers.

To further confuse things, a negative number next to accounts *payable* means your accounts payable balance went *down*. A positive number means your payables went *up*. Think about a $10,000 purchase you made from a supplier, you know, the one you promised to pay in 30 days "or so." The $10,000 purchase counted as expense but in effect, *you borrowed the $10,000* from your supplier to pay for it. Borrowing money from suppliers provides cash so your cash goes up when accounts payable go up and cash goes down when payables go down. You have more cash available when you borrow more of it from your suppliers.

On the one hand, a negative number means receivables went up, and on the other hand, a positive number means payables went down. It's no wonder people are frustrated trying to decipher the statement of cash flows but take heart. It all makes perfect sense in the end.

Shortcut

There is a shortcut for using the statement of cash flows report: look for the largest negative or positive number.

If the number is *negative*, say to yourself, for example, "Accounts receivable *consumed* $XXX of my cash." You have identified and quantified a cash problem. Then ask, "How did that happen?" You already know the answer to that question, and you can get to work changing your credit terms and speeding up collections.

If the number is positive, say to yourself, for example, "The note on my F-250 diesel truck provided $XXX cash." Then ask, "How is it that a bank loan on a truck *provided* cash?" You already know the answer to that question too—the bank loaned you some cash. Repeat the process for every significant number on the report and you will understand where your cash came from and where it went. That knowledge will place you squarely among an elite few business owners.

That's an overview of the statement of cash flows. The important things to know about it are:

1. The statement answers the question "Where did my cash go?"

2. If you have trouble understanding the report, it's not you. Everybody has trouble at first.

3. Like the income statement, the statement of cash flows is a period statement that shows where your cash went over a specific period of time.

4. You cannot produce an accurate statement of cash flows unless you keep books on an accrual basis.

5. Other than beginning and ending cash balances, the numbers on the report represent changes, not current balances.

6. Even if you don't understand the statement, you can use the following shortcut: For negative numbers, say to yourself, "This account consumed $XXX dollars of cash." For positive numbers, say to yourself, "This account provided $XXX dollars of cash."

Stay with it. Use the shortcut. Find the biggest numbers and ask your accountant what they mean. Keep asking until you understand. Once you're comfortable with the report, you'll laugh at how easy it is to understand and appreciate the valuable information it provides.

SECTION III

HOW TO USE
FINANCIAL REPORTS
TO MAKE
BETTER DECISIONS
AND MORE MONEY

CHAPTER 13

The Sixth Question: "What Should I Do?"

Immediately something like scales fell from his eyes, and he received his sight.

—Acts 9:18 (WEEBBE World English Bible British Edition)

Financial statements make management possible. Many of us, if we use them at all, use our financial statements to answer the five questions we saw earlier about our past or current condition. They are:

1. "Am I making money?"

2. "What do I own?"

3. "What do I owe?"

4. "What's left over for me?"

5. "Where did my cash go?"

We're interested in answers to those questions because we need to know how the score is kept and we, our lenders, investors, the IRS, and lots of other interested parties need to know what the score *is*. However, in your role as an owner, manager, and decision-maker, you should be keenly interested in a sixth question:

6.   "What should I do?"

The answer to that question will change your life, and you'll feel as Saul must have felt after arriving in Damascus: "I was blind, but now I see."

CHAPTER 14

Using the Income Statement

"There is no such thing as profit on an order or sale."

—Spencer A. Tucker,
   author of *The Break-Even System: A Tool for Profit Planning*

I N CHAPTER 10, I DESCRIBED THE INCOME STATEMENT AS HAVING THE MOST tactical value of the three financial statements. By that, I mean that you will use it most often to make decisions about the daily operations of your business. The decisions center on two critical concepts—margins and breakeven. In our discussion of the income statement, we will define both concepts, give examples of the astonishing number of uses for them, and show how immensely helpful they are for making decisions.

The Miracle of Breakeven

We saw in chapter 10 that in order to use your income statement to find breakeven, it has to be arranged properly. To understand why, look at the following income statement. This is a year-end income statement for Small Co. LLC. It's the same statement we saw in chapter 10 but with numbers.

Little Co LLC
Income Statement
January 1 – December 31, 20xx

Accrual Basis

Income

Job Income	$1,000,000
Total Income Assets	$1,000,000

Expenses

Direct Labor	300,000
Materials	300,000
Rent	50,000
Salaries	100,000
Interest	40,000
Insurance	50,000
Depreciation	30,000
Other	30,000
Total Expenses	**$900,000**
Net Income	**$100,000**

Most of the income statements I see in small businesses look pretty much like this one, with income at the top and all of the expenses listed below. The statement is straightforward and simple. It shows the business took in $1 million as sales, spent $900,000 on expenses, and earned a $100,000 profit. That much is clear, but based on this information, can it show you how much the company would have to sell to *exactly* pay all of its expenses? In other words, how much it would have to sell to break even on its operations?

I have asked that question to hundreds of small business owners, and the answer I hear most often is $900,000 from people looking at that report. That's a logical answer because total expenses are $900,000. Total sales of $900,000 minus total expenses of $900,000 equals zero and zero sounds a lot like breakeven. Unfortunately, it's not that simple. If sales dropped to $900,000, direct labor and material expense would also drop because they are variable expenses that go up and down with sales. The difference between $900,000 in sales and the new, lower expense number would no longer be zero.

"Okay," the usual thinking goes, "if expenses go down with reduced sales, I'll just reduce my guess to compensate," but that won't work either. If you reduce your guess below $900,000, labor and material expenses will go down again. Every time you reduce your guess for breakeven sales, labor and material expenses go down. This method has you chasing a moving target. You can see that it is difficult to find breakeven from even a simple income statement arranged like the one above.

Now look at the statement below. It contains the same information as the first one, only rearranged. You can see that the sales ($1 million) and net profit ($100,000) are the same, as are all of the individual expense items. The report just arrived at the $100,000 profit a little differently.

Little Co LLC
Income Statement
January 1 – December 31, 20xx

Accrual Basis

Income		% of Sales	
Job Income	$1,000,000	100%	
Total Income	**1,000,000**		
Cost of Goods Sold			
Direct Labor	300,000	30%	
Materials	300,000	30%	
Total Variable Costs	600,000	60%	
Gross Profit	**400,000**	**40%**	**Margin**
Fixed Expense			
Rent	50,000		
Salaries	100,000		
Vehicles	40,000		
Depreciations	50,000		
Insurance	30,000		
Office Expense	30,000		
Total Fixed Expenses	**300,000**	**30%**	
Net Income	**100,000**	**10%**	

In the rearranged statement, we moved direct labor and material expenses from overhead up to the new expense category called *cost of goods sold*, or *variable cost*. The move provides important new information.

You can now see that total variable cost is $600,000, gross profit is $400,000, and total overhead expense is $300,000. Other than that, the two statements report the same information.

The new information is important because it enables you to calculate those percentages shown on the right side of the report. Each one represents the adjacent number as a percentage of sales.[27] The percentage in which we are most interested is margin, the number next to Gross Profit on the income statement above. Margin is *gross profit expressed as a percentage of sales*.

In this example, the number is:

40%

And there it is: Margin—the most important number in business operations—which in this example is 40 percent. The sole purpose for rearranging your income statements is to get to that number. You cannot do any of the calculations you will see below without it. You *must* know this number for your business.

Think of margin as *your share of the sales dollar* because it is. In order to produce a dollar of sales, for example, Small Co. LLC has to spend 60 cents in variable expenses. That's true for the first dollar of sales, the next dollar, and every dollar after that.[28] The 40-cent margin that remains after paying variable expense is all that's left to pay overhead and, after all overhead has been paid, to accumulate as profit. You have probably heard people talk about the great "profit" they made on this sale or that job but it's not so. You do not earn any *profit* until you have first recovered all of your expenses, including overhead. Then (and only then) do margins begin to accumulate as

---

27 QuickBooks will calculate the percentages for you with one click of the mouse.
28 There is a point at which variable costs change due to changes in the scale of our operations, but we're not going to worry about that right now.

net profit. This is what Spencer Tucker meant when he said, "*There is no such thing as profit on an order or sale*"—only margins (hopefully).

Margins are the most important numbers in business operations because they enable you to calculate different types of breakeven, which inform an astonishing number of decisions. Margins teach you how expenses actually behave, which leads to better decisions and more money.

For some people, the arithmetic is easy and why it works is obvious. For others, it's not that simple. Many people would rather disarm live hand grenades with their bare feet than even think about math. For those who fall into the latter category, the 1% rule should provide incentive to continue:

The 1% rule says that increasing gross profit margins by 1 percent of sales (for example, from 40 percent to 41 percent) will increase net profits by 14.5 percent.

Interested? I will show why it works in the last paragraph of this chapter. In the meantime, let's get started and see how margins and breakeven work.

First, what is breakeven and why should you care about it?

Breakeven is the amount you must sell to generate a target amount of gross profit. The target could be the amount required to pay all of your overhead, to pay all of your overhead *plus* a budgeted net profit, to pay for an increase in a certain expense, to find the effects of price changes, or to decide whether to buy a piece of equipment, and so on. There is a breakeven component to every business decision you make.

When most of us hear the term *breakeven*, we think of overall breakeven. That's the point at which you have sold enough to pay all your expenses with no net loss or profit. It's also the point at which you have sold enough to begin making a profit. Understanding how much you have to sell to reach overall breakeven is the first and most fundamental breakeven question. Every single one of us should know that number for our companies.

Calculating overall breakeven is easy once you know your overhead and margins: simply divide total overhead by margin.

On Small Co. LLC's income statement, overhead is $300,000 and margin is 40 percent; therefore, overall breakeven for the company is:

$$\$300,000 \text{ total overhead expense} / \$0.40 \text{ margin}$$
$$= \$750,000 \text{ overall breakeven}$$

The company breaks even when it reaches $750,000 in sales. One more dollar of sales would earn the company a 40-cent net profit. One dollar less, and the company would suffer a 40-cent loss.

Their income statement shows Small Co. LLC sold $1 million last year, which is $250,000 more than breakeven sales of $750,000. The margin on the extra $250,000 contributes entirely to profit, which means the company earned $100,000 in net profit, which matches the net profit on their income statement.

$$\$250,000 \text{ sales above breakeven} \times \$0.40 \text{ margin}$$
$$= \$100,000 \text{ net profit}$$

All of that is interesting but why should you care?

First, you should care because understanding breakeven disciplines your thinking and efforts. My conversations with hundreds of small business owners suggest that most go to work on the first day of each month believing everybody makes a little money that day, and the next, and the next after that. Every day, you make a little profit, your employees make their wages, your landlord makes some rent, your suppliers, insurance providers, utility companies, and all the people with whom you do business earn their daily cut. But *noooo!* That's not true.

Although you may earn *revenue* every day, you do not make any money—nothing, not even a tiny whiff of profit—until you have paid all the bills for the month and that doesn't happen until you reach breakeven sales. It's dangerous to think otherwise because if you don't break even until the 29th of the month, you had better not go fishing on the 30th. If you do, you forfeit your last opportunity to earn a net profit before all those monthly bills reset on the first of next month.

The second reason you should care is that breakeven transforms the question "How much does it cost?" into "How much do I have to sell to pay for it?" The difference is more than semantics. The rephrased question focuses your attention on the fact that you have little influence over the cost of your purchases but you have a great deal of influence over how much you have to sell to pay for them. Yes, yes, I know, controlling expense is always important but life isn't that simple. You can't merely save your way to prosperity. If it were that easy, you could just close your business, shed *all* your expenses, and get rich. We both know that won't work. You have to spend money to make money, and the challenge is to get the most in return for the money you spend.

An hour of labor, a square foot of shop space, and a pallet of material costs pretty much the same for everyone competing in the same market. In spite of that, some people flourish while others languish.

As I write this, I'm coaching three contractors who work in the same trade.[29] Their shops are located within 10 miles of each other and they do the same kind of work in the same market. The three are about the same age with about the same experience. They buy their material from the same supply houses and draw their labor from the same labor pool. As a result, all three bid jobs for about the same prices and pay the same for both material and labor. There are a lot more similarities among them, but as you can see below, there are some big differences as well.

Last year's sales for the three were as follows:

Contractor A: $460,000
Contractor B: $610,000
Contractor C: $2.8 million

---

29 As a business coach, I generally do not work with clients who directly compete with each other. These three are exceptions. They know each other and they know I work with all of them. This a great group of guys who adhere to an abundance mindset. They often help each other and believe there is more than enough work to go around.

Last year's net profit as a percentage of sales for the three were:

Contractor A: 5 percent
Contractor B: 20 percent
Contractor C: 1 percent

Let that last part sink in.

Contractor A made a net profit of $20,500 on $460,000 of sales;
Contractor B made a net profit of $122,000 on $610,000 of sales; and
Contractor C made a net profit of $ 28,000 on $2.8 million sales.

Contractor B made two-and-a-half times as much as A and B combined and he did it on less than one-fifth of their combined total sales.

So why is it that Contractor B flourishes while Contractors A and C struggle?[30] The first reason is that he has a good grasp of the purpose of business. He is after margin, profit, and cash rather than sales for the sake of sales. There are other reasons as well but chief among them is that he keeps good books and knows his margins and his breakeven sales. He bids jobs to earn a 40 percent margin (or more) and he keeps his overhead to 20 percent or less of sales. He and his employees constantly track the numbers to be sure they are on time and on budget, and they take corrective action if they see they are going astray.

Contractor B has learned to get more in return for what he spends. Instead of focusing entirely on what things cost, he concentrates on spreading overhead costs over higher sales, getting more production from each dollar of labor, eliminating waste, and using materials more efficiently. He concentrates on what he can influence most and is more productive than his peers. As a result, he earns higher margins, which lead to lower breakeven sales, which lead to higher net profits achieved earlier each month, which leads to more time to earn even more profit.

---

30 Contractors A and C are struggling for the time being. They are working hard to get their net profits up, and I have no doubt that they will. Contractor B has provided them both inspiration and proof that it can be done.

Using Margins and Breakeven to Make Decisions

Thinking in terms of breakeven rather than cost is fundamental to improving productivity. A breakeven mentality influences productivity by focusing your attention on the things over which you have the most control. It suggests actions you can take to improve the future and it tells you how well your past decisions worked. The information is made visible by one simple, powerful number: your breakeven sales.

Breakeven has many uses, including:

1. To find how much you must sell to pay all or part of a particular expense

2. To find how much you must sell to pay all of your expenses, plus earn a budgeted profit

3. To analyze different compensation packages

4. To pay for a new vehicle or piece of equipment

5. To earn enough to pay total expenses *and* debt payments

6. To evaluate buying a new production machine

7. To tell you how much more you have to sell if you reduce your prices

8. To demonstrate the amazing power of small changes

9. To tell you how much less you can sell if you increase your prices

10. To find out how much you have to sell to double your profit

11. To engage and incentivize your team

12. To help establish prices for products and bids

13. To locate and fix production problems

14. To show you how to build houses for free (WHAT? See page 144)

The applications are endless. You've already seen how to find overall breakeven. Let's look at how breakeven informs individual decisions. For example, let's assume your income statement is the same as the earlier example and use breakeven to answer some common questions.

Q: How much do salespeople have to sell to pay for themselves?

In order to grow, you've decided you need to hire a salesperson. The going rate for a decent salesperson in your industry and area is $5,000 per month. That's a lot of money for a company your size and you hesitate. You know what an additional $5,000 of expense each month will do to your cash but have no idea what the salesperson will bring in or how much they have to sell to at least recover the cost of their salary.

A: This is a classic decision confronting small business owners: Should you hire the salesperson? Would it be useful to know *in advance* how much they must sell to break even on the additional cost of their salary?

A new monthly salary of $5,000 adds $5,000 per month to the overhead; therefore:

$5,000 salary / $0.40 commission = $12,500 breakeven.

Hiring the salesperson would increase your breakeven sales by $12,500. You now have some useful information. Is it reasonable in your business to expect a salesperson to sell at least $12,500 per month? Does that information add perspective to the hiring decision?

Q: How much would new salespeople have to sell to pay for themselves *and* produce a target gross profit?

A: None of us hire salespeople to swap dollars. We hire them to make money. How much must the salesperson sell to both pay for themselves and bring in *an additional* $10,000 of gross profit each month? The target now is $5,000 to recover their salary plus $10,000 of additional gross profit, for a total of $15,000.

$$\$15,000 \text{ target} / \$0.40 \text{ margin} = \$37,500 \text{ breakeven}$$

The salesperson would have to sell $37,500 each month to pay for themselves and generate a $10,000 gross profit. You can use that information to evaluate the hiring decision. Is $37,500 per month a reasonable expectation? How long might it take a new hire to reach that level of sales? Would that information be useful for setting sales quotas and expectations?

Q: How much would salespeople have to sell to pay for themselves with a compensation package of base pay plus commission?

A: Most of us are uncomfortable paying salespeople a guaranteed monthly salary. We want them to have an incentive to get out there and produce. Let's say that instead of a guaranteed $5,000 per month salary, you choose to offer a $3,000 salary and 10 percent (of sales) commission. Is that a good idea? (By the way, a lot of us land on 10 percent because it's a nice round number and easy to blurt out. However, for most businesses, a commission of 10 percent of sales would be a huge burden.[31])

The salesperson's target now is their $3,000 salary plus $10,000 of additional gross profit, for a total of $13,000. Their 10 percent commission, however, increases variable costs, which reduce your margin from 40 percent to 30 percent. The salesman now has to hit their target with a lower margin.

$$\$13,000 \text{ target} / \$0.30 \text{ margin} = \$43,333 \text{ breakeven}$$

This commission pay package would reduce your risk because you guaranteed only $3,000 per month instead of $5,000. However, it increased your breakeven from $37,500 to $43,333. Would you be happy with that trade-off?

When evaluating the pay package, you would also have to consider how the commission would affect your gross profit beyond breakeven. For exam-

---

31 The discussion below on discounts shows the dramatic effects of a 10% decrease in your margins. Commissions are not price discounts but they have the same effect: both reduce margins.

ple, assume your salesperson sold $100,000 worth of product in one month. Under the salary-only plan, their fixed compensation would be $5,000, your company would make $40,000 gross profit, and your net benefit would be $35,000. Under the base pay/commission plan, their fixed compensation would be $3,000, your company would make $30,000 gross profit, and your net benefit would be $27,000.

$100,000 sales with salary-only plan:

$100,000 sales x $0.40 margin = $40,000 gross profit
$40,000 gross profit - $5,000 salary = $35,000 net benefit to the company

$100,000 sales with base pay plus 10 percent commission:

$100,000 sales x $0.30 margin = $30,000 gross profit
$30,000 gross profit - $3,000 base salary = $27,000 gross profit

Does the reduced risk of a lower salary compensate for the increased risk of a higher breakeven? Does the reduced risk of a lower salary justify a commission that would rise continually with increasing sales? Would this information be useful to have *in advance* of offering a commission-based compensation package to a salesperson?

Q: How much more do you have to sell to pay for a new truck?

I live in Oklahoma, and some of the more noticeable features of life here are severe spring thunderstorms. The storms bring the kind of heavy rain, large hail, and damaging winds that annihilate roofs and torment insurance adjusters. As surely as spring flowers follow the rain so do roofing contractors follow the hail. In areas hit by significant hail, new contractors blossom more quickly than the flowers, with many of them sporting fancy new trucks wrapped with graphics touting their newly organized LLCs. They are everywhere, and I might see as many as 20 per hour driving through my neighborhood. There is nothing wrong with their creating companies to take advantage of an opportunity. In fact, I respect their initiative. However, I can drive down my street and predict who will be in business in a year. How do I know? Their trucks. A brand-new $100,000 F-250 Ford diesel with a $3,000 wrap job pulling a new $15,000 trailer is an almost certain indication of early demise. It happens because the new contractors are flush with revenue but don't know about margins or the sales required to break even on the new rig.

A: So what does it take to break even on the new $118,000 rig? With the 20 percent margins common to the industry, they will have to sell:

$118,000 / $0.20 margin = $590,000 breakeven on the truck

They will have to sell and collect $590,000 worth of roofing jobs just to break even on the nominal cost of the truck and that's before interest, insurance, operating and repair costs, and the rest of the overhead associated with the roofing business.

Q: How about you? Maybe you don't need a $118,000 rig. You'd be perfectly happy with a $75,000 F-150 Platinum series. You've convinced yourself it's a good price because you can finance it for less than $1,000 per month (and because you really, really want it). But regardless of financing, with a 40 percent margin, you still have to generate additional sales of $187,000 to break even on the cost of the truck:

$75,000 cost of truck / $0.40 margins = $187,000 breakeven sales

A: Wow, $187,000 is less than $590,000 but it's still a lot of money. The price looks different in terms of breakeven, doesn't it? Will the truck increase your productivity by $187,000 (or more)? How badly do you *need* the truck? How badly do you *want* it? Would that knowledge affect your definition of a reasonable price? Is there a less expensive alternative?

Q: How much do you have to sell to pay all expenses *and* your debt payments?

If you're like most business owners, you have debt (especially if you just bought a new truck), which means you have payments due each month on your vehicle and equipment loans, your mortgage, and your operating loan. We saw in chapter 10 that repayment of debt is not an expense.[32] That means that if you earn enough gross profit just to break even on expenses, you still haven't earned enough to pay all of your bills, which include debt service payments.

A: How much would you have to sell to pay all your overhead plus your monthly debt service? Assume that your monthly overhead is $30,000 and your monthly debt payments total another $10,000. That means your gross profit target is $40,000 and your sales target is $100,000.

$$(\$30,000 \text{ overhead} + \$10,000 \text{ debt service}) / \$0.40 \text{ margin}$$
$$= \$100,000 \text{ sales target}$$

You begin making a profit at $30,000 / $0.40 = $75,000 sales but don't earn enough profit to make all your debt payments until sales reach $100,000. (Even then, you may not be out of the woods because you can't repay debt with profit, only cash, and just because you make money doesn't mean you have any. That is the key message of this book.)

Q: Should you buy that new machine?

An equipment salesperson, doing what good salespeople do, tells you about a new CNC machine that will automate a process and reduce your labor costs from 30 percent to 20 percent of sales. If that were true, your total margin would increase from 40 percent to 50 percent, which is a significant increase and worth investigating. The supplier offers to lease the machine to you for $4,500 per month. The 10 percent increase in margins is really attractive but the lease expense adds $4,500 per month to overhead and that's a lot of money. Should you lease the machine?

A: In a case like this, you should plan to recover the $4,500 through the 10

---

32 Recall that what you bought with debt may (or may not) have been an expense but repayment of debt is not. All debt is repaid from profits.

percent improvement that can be attributed entirely to the machine. How much do you have to sell to break even on the machine?

$4,500 new overhead cost / $0.10 increase in margin
= $45,000 sales to break even

That means that at $45,000 monthly sales, the machine has paid its way. It's generating enough new margin to pay for itself. But again, you're not interested in swapping dollars. What happens if your sales go up more than $45,000? For every dollar of sales over $45,000, you would earn 10 cents more than you would without the machine. If you can muster $90,000 in sales, the machine would pay for itself *and* generate another $4,500 in gross profit. That looks like a pretty good investment. Your question then becomes: How likely is it that the machine will actually reduce labor costs? How likely are we to sell $45,000 or $90,000 or some other amount each month? Is the potential prize worth the certain risk of committing to the lease? Breakeven can't answer those questions but it gives you reasons to examine things more closely or to abandon the idea.

General Application

We could go on and on with specific examples but you get the idea. We answered all the questions using the same method:

Target gross profit / % margin
= Sales required to generate the target gross profit

The general method applies to all breakeven decisions. Suppose you want to move to a more expensive office. Divide the increase in rent by your percentage margin to find the breakeven sales necessary to pay for the increase. Then ask yourself, "Would the move generate sufficient sales to justify the cost?" Suppose you want to buy new computers, increase your marketing budget, or raise your office salaries. Same thing. Divide the increase in overhead by margin to find the breakeven sales figure. Once you get the number, ask yourself if sales are likely to increase enough that gross profit *at least* covers the increased cost.

You should know your margins and carry the number in your head at all times. That way, you can quickly calculate breakeven to make better decisions about choices that affect cost. And, by the way, all business decisions affect cost.

Breakeven is a pretty straightforward, useful concept but it's even more powerful than we've seen so far. You can also use it to answer other interesting but more complex questions.

Q: How much more do you have to sell to break even on discounted prices?

A: I learned a lesson from my hobby that I'll never forget. I'm a business coach by trade but I'm also an amateur painter. At my very first public show, I noticed a lady who had twice visited my exhibit and was back for the third time contemplating a large oil painting. As I approached her, I said, "I know what you're thinking."

"Oh?" she responded. "What's that?"

"You're thinking that's a lot of money for a painting. How about I knock 20 percent off the price?"

"Thanks," she said. "I'll take it. But just so you know, I was thinking about how to get it home. I measured and it won't fit in my car."

Ouch!

She got a nice painting (I delivered it) and I got a valuable lesson: our hang-ups about price are almost always our own head trash.

Can you relate? Do you discount your prices? Why? Have you ever had an experience like mine? I've asked hundreds of business owners and managers why they discount their prices. The answers almost always[33] come down to the same thing: They discount to attract more sales. If the purpose of discounts is to attract more sales, wouldn't it make sense to know *in advance* how much more you have to sell to *at least* break even on the cost of the discounts? That's one of the most intelligent questions I've never been asked. The answer will inform and influence your decisions and might even persuade you to find ways other than discounting to attract new business.

A: You can find exactly how much more business you have to attract to compensate for discounts by comparing changes in margins at various discount levels to changes in breakeven.[34] The calculation is more complex than the one we've been using so far because you have to compare two related variables: The margin before discounts and the margin after discounts. The calculation rises from simple arithmetic to algebra so we'll replace the math with a table and some examples.

We probably agree that there's nothing remarkable about a marketing promotion that offers customers a 20 percent discount as an incentive to buy. Twenty percent doesn't seem like such a big deal. Besides, what harm could it do, as long as it brings in some more business? That's a good question. What's your guess? How much more do you suppose you would have to sell to recover the cost of a 20 percent price reduction? Before you understood margins, you might have been tempted to guess that a 20 percent increase in sales would do it but you've seen enough by now to know that's probably not the answer. And you're right, it's not. We will use margins and breakeven to find the exact answer. You may be surprised.

Look at the table below. The percentages across the columns at the top are pre-discount gross profit margins. The percentages down the left side are

---

33 Discounting is a legitimate tool for reducing obsolete inventory (in other words, for correcting previous inventory mistakes). Discounting can also be an effective strategy to acquire customers, as long as the lifetime value of the customer is significantly greater than the cost of discount. In either case, it's always worthwhile to understand the effects of discounting and to explore alternatives before resorting to price concessions.

34 Visit the website at www.TheProfitProblem.com and download my free discount and price increase calculators. The calculators tell you how much your sales must go up or can go down to maintain profit levels after discounts or price increases.

various possible discounts percentages. To find the impact of a 20 percent discount on a company with 40 percent margins, look at the intersection of the 40 percent column and the 20 percent row. The number there is 100 percent, which is the amount your sales would have to increase just to recover the cost of the 20 percent discount.

	35%	40%
10%	40%	33%
12%	52%	43%
14%	67%	54%
16%	84%	67%
18%	106%	82%
20%	133%	100%
25%	250%	167%
30%	600%	300%

Yikes! Say it out loud: "Sales would have to go up 100 percent—or double—just to maintain the gross profit I already have." That's a high bar to hurdle. Even if you pulled it off, you would find yourself working twice as hard for the same total gross profit. You can see on the chart that a 30 percent discount would require tripling sales just to keep profit the same! Is working harder for the same or less what you had in mind when you thought up that innocent-sounding discount promotion?

The dramatic effect of discounts may not be obvious but it makes perfect sense. Remember, margins are your share of a sales dollar. The damaging effect of discounting is due to the fact that *discounts come entirely from your share.* After all, just because you chose to discount doesn't mean your suppliers reduced their bills or your employees agreed to work for less.

Q: On the flip side, how much less could you sell without reducing profit if you raised your prices?

Businesses discount because they want to attract more customers. They are reluctant to raise prices because they are afraid to lose customers. Do you agree with that statement? Have you raised your prices? Why or why not? If you did, what happened?

A: The Belgian beer Stella Artois created a famous ad campaign around the slogan "Reassuringly Expensive." The campaign was a great success because those two words resonate with all of us. You understand *precisely* what they mean, don't you?[35]

If you constantly look for examples of a price increase that cost you this or that customer, you'll find them. But if you look for examples of "reassuringly expensive," you'll find those too. It took me fewer than five minutes to compile the following examples from client companies.

The first is from a general contractor who, among other things, has refurbished over 50 burnt-out homes. He recently received three bids from subcontractors for a new project. The spread between the high and low bids was over $100,000. He chose the highest bid because, as he told me, "The low guys would be coming back for more money, or they'd walk off the job. I took the high bid because I know I will be a priority for the contractor, and I know the job will get done." That decision is the voice of experience. The high bid was reassuringly expensive.

The second is from a client business that sells replacement windows. The owner came to our coaching session on a Friday afternoon totally frustrated. He had lost a job to a competitor that priced the same quality windows for just over 500 percent more than his bid. Five times as much! No kidding. The homeowner took the higher bid and explained to my client that she "didn't want to go cheap with my home." My client was on the wrong end of reassuringly expensive.

The third example involves electrical contractor C from the earlier example. His company earns about 30 percent of its revenue from residential and

---

35 In his bestselling book, *Influence,* Robert D. Cialdini, PhD describes our tendency to judge quality by price as a "shortcut" we use to avoid brain strain in an increasingly complex world.

commercial service work, with the balance coming from new commercial construction jobs. We spent our coaching session discussing price increases and talking about how small price increases can have a huge impact on net profit. We were talking about the information contained in this section of this book. Predictably, he was reluctant to raise prices because he was afraid to lose customers—at least he was until we reviewed the table below. The table showed that with his 35 percent margins and a 10 percent price increase, he could lose 22 percent of his business without sacrificing any gross profit. He was convinced. He went back to his office that afternoon and raised his hourly rate for a two-person service crew from $95 to $135 per hour! That's a 42 percent increase! I usually don't advocate for such dramatic change but it worked for him. As of this writing, it has been five months since the price increase. He has earned an extra $120,000 of gross profit and only one customer has mentioned the price increase but he paid. Contractor C knows I'm using him as an example in this book and, after raising his prices, he asked that from now on I refer to him as "Contractor $." Done.[36]

So what is it about a contractor who bids $100,000 more than the competition, a window company that has the guts to ask five times more than his competitors, or a contractor who raises his rates 42 percent in one fell swoop? They have all reached a sophisticated level of confidence that, at least in part, is due to understanding margins.

Among the most predictable challenges I have with new clients is persuading them to raise prices, even by a few percentage points on a few select items. The most common excuses I hear are, "My competitors will slaughter me," "The market won't bear an increase," and "I can't raise *her* prices because she refers a lot of business to us."

I don't recall ever hearing a client say, "I won't raise prices because I tested higher prices for three months, measured the results, and my profits dropped." There are two reasons I haven't heard that. The first is that very

---

36 Since I first wrote this paragraph, contractor $ raised his prices by another 18 percent. None of his clients have even mentioned the price increase to him.

few business owners have tested higher prices and measured the results, and the second is that when prices go up, more often than not, so do profits.

It takes courage to raise prices and overcome the fear of losing customers. The antidote is confidence that comes from two main sources. The first is a well-defined unique selling proposition, or USP, that emphasizes the reasons, other than price, that customers buy from you. The second is information that tells you what would happen if you were to lose customers. Regarding the first problem, I've provided a downloadable workbook to help create your USP at www.TheProfitProblem.com.

The table below answers the second problem by showing you what would happen if you were to lose customers to higher prices.

	35%	40%
4%	10%	9%
8%	19%	17%
10%	22%	20%
14%	29%	26%
16%	31%	29%
20%	36%	33%

The table tells us how much business we could lose at various levels of price increases before lower sales would reduce our profit.

Read this table the same way you read the last one. The difference between the two is that the numbers in this table show how much business *you could lose* before the loss of sales reduced your profit. For example, if you have a 40 percent margin and are considering a 10 percent price increase, follow the 40 percent column down to its intersection with the 10 percent row. The number there is 20 percent. That tells you that you could lose 20 percent of your sales before your gross profit would decline. To find out what would happen with a 20 percent price increase, follow the 40 percent column down to the 20 percent row. You will see that you could lose one-third (33 percent) of your sales without sacrificing a penny of profit.

Does that information give you courage? I hope so, because even if 20 percent of your customers abandoned you due to a 10 percent price increase, you would make the same profit as before while working 20 percent less. But that won't happen. Most of my clients' customers don't even notice a 10 percent price increase, let alone jump ship in response. The few customers who leave are generally of the price-shopping, late-paying, complaint-making, warranty-busting, call-you-at-home-on-the-weekend variety you would be better off without. Send them to competitors and benefit twice!

However, if none of your customers left, you would be stuck doing the *same* amount of work but you would earn an extra 10 percent gross profit on every dollar of sales. A price increase has a much greater impact on gross profit than simply increasing sales volume because higher sales volume also means higher variable costs. With higher *prices*, income goes up *without increasing costs*. It's kind of like free money that goes straight to net profit. If you can find a way to increase both sales volume and prices, you will be shocked by the results!

Q: How much more would you have to sell to double your net profit?

A: "What would it take to double your profit?"

I was talking to Aaron, a contractor whose company clears vegetation from rights-of-way for railroads, pipelines, power lines, and other public and private entities. It's a tough business that should reward the owner with ample profit to justify the risk and effort. About a month before I asked that question, we asked his accountant to properly rearrange his QuickBooks files. When the accountant returned the files, Aaron's margins were visible for the first time.

"What do you mean?" Aaron asked.

"I mean, based on last year, how much more would you have had to sell to double your net profit?"

"I don't know. Probably not double but something close to that."

"How about 10.8 percent?"

"You're *kidding* me," he answered. "Are you telling me that if I had sold 10 percent more, it would have doubled my net profit last year?"

"Well, actually 10.8 percent, but yes."

"How do you figure that?"

That's a great question. Once you know how to figure it out, you can easily get answers to that and a lot of other interesting and useful questions. The answers transform your managerial assumptions (such as assuming you'd have to work twice as hard to double your profit) into informed decisions that have a huge impact on profit.

"If you had known that, do you think you could have sold 10 percent more?" I asked.

"You're damn right," Aaron answered.

This is the miracle of breakeven (of course, it's not a miracle; it just seems like it). You're slogging away, paying everyone else. Then one day, you hit breakeven and *bam*! You start to make money and it begins to pile up at an astonishing rate. The danger is not understanding how breakeven works and slacking off just when you should be doubling down on your efforts.

We will see exactly how a 10.8 percent increase in sales would have doubled Aaron's profit in the next paragraph, but in the meantime, do you know how much more you have to sell to double your profit? Why does that question matter? Could you have sold 10 percent more if it would have doubled your net profit? Why didn't you? If you're like Aaron and a lot of us, the reason you didn't is because you didn't realize such a small change could have such a disproportionate impact. Maybe you're laboring under the notion that you would have to double your efforts to double your net profit. You're already tired and just the thought of working twice as much exhausts you.

Although it's not the same for every business, my experience has shown that most small businesses could double their net profit by increasing their sales by 10 to 20 percent if they keep their margins and overhead the same. Understanding margins and breakeven is the key to understanding why and how that happens. Understanding provides incentive to make those changes and gives us an alternative to the gut decisions we have all lived to regret.

Now to Aaron's question: Based on his business last year, how much more would he have had to sell to double his net profit? For this one, we'll use his actual income statement. The target is to double his $160,000 net profit. How did I know a 10.8 percent increase in sales would do it? His income statement looked like this:

Aaron's Income Statement

Sales	$3,700,000	100%
Variable costs	$2,220,000	60%
Gross profit	**$1,480,000**	**40%**
Fixed costs	$1,320,000	
Net profit	**$160,000**	

Aaron's company was past breakeven, which meant margins from new sales would all accumulate as profit. Doubling his profit meant he had to earn another $160,000. To see how much more he would have to sell to do that, we use the formula for generating a target gross profit:

$160,000 target gross profit / $0.40 margin = $400,000 new sales

The $400,000 of new sales are 10.8 percent of his original $3.7 million sales.

$400,000 new sales / $3,700,000 original sales = 10.8%

Therefore, Aaron's sales would have to increase 10.8 percent in order to increase his profit from $160,000 to $320,000.

Q: When we start thinking about margins, we can find all sorts of uses for them. For example, what would happen if Aaron increased his margins from 40 percent to 45 percent?

$3,700,000 sales x $0.05 increase in margin = $185,000 additional profit

A: His sales of $3.7 million times 5 percent means that a 45 percent margin would generate an additional $185,000 of gross profit. Because he's already above breakeven, the entire $185,000 would flow to the bottom line, more than doubling his net profit!

Q: What if he could raise sales 10.8 percent *and* increase margins 5 percent? His income statement would now look like this:

Aaron's Income Statement

Sales	$4,100,000	100%
Variable costs	$2,255,000	55%
Gross profit	**$1,845,000**	**45%**
Fixed costs	$1,320,000	
Net profit	**$525,000**	

A: If Aaron could increase his sales by 10 percent *and* raise his margins from 40 percent to 45 percent, his profit would rise from $160,000 to $525,000— an increase of 325 percent!

How can I get the point across to my people?

One of my favorite books on leadership, and one I fully recommend, is *Turn the Ship Around!* by Captain L. David Marquet. It's a fascinating story about a hapless US nuclear submarine, the *USS Santa Fe*, that was ranked last in many performance categories by the US Navy. Captain Marquet was assigned to the ship unexpectedly but managed to transform the *Santa Fe* into one of the finest ships in the navy.

The book is about leadership, not margins, but one of the compelling points Captain Marquet makes is that we, nuclear sub captains, business owners, managers, and leaders have the *authority* but our people—our teams—have the *power*. To some degree at least, we all sit in our offices or board rooms to pontificate about the power of margins and breakeven and the importance of targets and goals. All the while, our teams are out executing—or not—to transform our plans into reality. Our fates are in their hands. For that reason, at a bare minimum, our people must understand and buy into the power and effects of margins and breakeven.

Kevin, a contractor client of mine, confronted Marquet's authority/power issue. Kevin had worked nine years as a journeyman electrician for other electrical contractors. The year before we met, he got his contractor's license and started his own shop. His ambition, as he described it very simply and clearly, was to "take off his tool belt." He envisioned a personal future free of 140-degree summertime attics and cold, wet, wintertime construction sites. He also looked forward to earning dividends from a profitable company and spending more time with his wife and family. That was the idea, anyway.

Over the first three years I knew him, his sales tripled each year, from five digits the first year to near seven digits in the third year. That's a pretty good increase from the bidding and sales perspective. Kevin was making great progress but there was a problem. He was bleeding cash and he wasn't making much money.

Kevin is a smart, capable electrical contractor but he's also compassionate—maybe too much so. He had suffered as an employee under business owners he considered to be tyrannical, severe bosses. He was determined to treat his employees with respect, which in practice meant that he allowed them great latitude in setting their work schedules. Maybe you can guess where this is going.

We usually think of breakeven as a monthly target we have to hit in order to begin making a net profit. It's logical to think in terms of a monthly breakeven because most of our fixed expenses recur on a monthly basis. However, it's sometimes useful to divide our monthly fixed expenses by the days in the month to come up with a target daily breakeven sales number.

We started with breakeven to understand why Kevin wasn't making money. Instead of using a monthly breakeven number, we divided his monthly overhead by the number of days worked to find a *daily* breakeven number for individual electricians. It turned out that each electrician had to work seven hours per day for the company to break even. The eighth hour was the profit hour. As you probably have guessed, the guys averaged fewer than seven hours per day. They worked enough hours to cover the cost of their wages, materials, and shop overhead but not a single hour for profit. They had no idea that they were harming the company by taking off early every day (well, maybe some of them did). They reasoned that they weren't getting paid so what's the harm? The harm, of course, was that margins for the eighth hour would have gone entirely to profit.

We met with the employees and introduced the concept of breakeven and showed them, using Kevin's actual numbers, why the company needed at least eight hours every day from every electrician. Kevin laid out a new standard that required everyone to average at least eight hours per day. After a few difficult months of employee turnover (some of them weren't happy about working a full 40 hours per week), he's now on solid footing, earning consistent profits. He also has a newfound appreciation for the tyrannical behavior of his old boss.

How can margins motivate my team?

Although it was almost 50 years ago, I remember listening as a teenager to a discussion between my father, John Holland, and a brilliant consultant, Helmut Goerling. My father was an inventor with many patents to his credit who had created a highly successful manufacturing company. He sat at our dining room table talking to Helmut, and I sat across from them, happy to be there, listening intently.

My father and Helmut talked about how to increase production of my father's newest paving equipment.[37] The great advantage of the machine was that it enabled paving contractors to dramatically reduce variable costs and earn much higher margins on asphalt paving jobs. Contractors who realized the advantage[38] of the machine simply had to have it, and the sooner the better. The orders were rolling in, and they needed to figure out how to keep up with demand.

After an hour of discussion, my father and Helmut hit upon an idea. One of the main limitations to production was labor. If they were going to increase production significantly without adding a lot of plant capacity and people, they were going to have to find ways to reduce labor costs as a percentage of sales.

"We're going to have the guys in the plant help us figure this out," my father said. "We will make a deal with them. For every dollar of labor they remove from the cost of a machine, we'll give them half the saving as a bonus, and we'll use the other half to buy more efficient tools and equipment."

To my 16-year-old brain, that sounded like a horrible idea.

"Why would you do that?" I asked. "What's in it for you if they come up

---

37 The machine was called the Flowboy and was the first horizontal-discharge, live-bottom, asphalt-hauling trailer. There are many copycats now that the patents have expired, and horizontal-discharge trailers are standard on most large paving jobs.

38 The Flowboy could reduce variable costs for asphalt paving by as much as 20 percent. My father and Dr. Goerling marketed the machine by *teaching paving contractors about margins and breakeven,* which were novel ideas in 1969. Contractors who understood the concepts almost always and almost immediately purchased Flowboys.

with a bunch of savings and you either give it to them or spend it on tools? There's nothing left for you." I remember my father smiling and patting me on the shoulder.

"You'll see," he said. And boy, did I.

The employees in the plant came up with ideas and processes that increased their production rate from 30 units per year to a rate of 300 units per year, and they did it in 12 months! (They were a remarkable group of employees.) The company did not immediately benefit directly from higher margins because it spent the savings, but over the first year, it earned standard margins on 10 times as many units. Over the second and subsequent years, it reaped the benefits of the *higher margins* times the *higher production*! The plan was an astonishing success.

My father knew and understood the variable labor cost of manufacturing his machines. That knowledge provided the information with which he could devise a plan and measure and reward improvements. Without it, the program would not have been possible.

Using Margins to Make More Money

When you begin, as my father did, to think in terms of margins and breakeven, you begin to see things you didn't notice before and to think differently. I had a conversation recently with a CPA who collaborates with me in setting up clients with proper books. She understands that the highest and best use of good books is to make decisions about the future. She knows how to calculate and use margins and breakeven. She understands the power of small changes.

Still, she asked, "I see on paper all these great things that will happen if my clients improve margins but what do I tell them to do? I've never been a contractor, manufacturer, retailer, or anything other than a CPA. How am I supposed to know what they can *actually do* to increase margins?" That's a valid question.

My answer was and is that I don't always know what to do, *but my clients do.* Once we focus, for example, on reducing labor cost as a percentage of sales, we put our heads together and we *always* find ways to do it.

There are two approaches to reducing expenses as a percentage of sales. One is to get the same for less so you work to keep gross profit the same while cutting expenses. The other is to get more for the same so you work to get more gross profit from the expenses you already have. My clients generally emphasize the getting more from the same approach. Of course, you can always do both!

Getting it done in practice requires four things:

1. We have to choose and measure the result we want to improve (see chapter 21: "KPIs").

2. We have to fully grasp and believe in the power of small changes, which enables us to establish target improvements we can achieve.

3. We need to quantify the potential benefits of change.

4. We have to generate some ideas,[39] implement them, and measure the effects.

The best way to show you how it works is with real-life examples.

Example 1: Parts Off the Truck

This clever idea is one of my favorites.

Recall the three electrical contractors we met earlier. Contractor $ (formerly Contractor C) earned a paltry $28,000 net profit last year on $2.8 million in sales. To say he was not pleased with that result is an understatement.

At year-end, Contractor $ was doing three kinds of electrical work: New commercial construction, new homes, and service work (both residential and commercial). It took almost three months to get his books arranged so that

---

39 I recommend reading *2 Second Lean* by Paul Akers. The book is about manufacturing, but lean principles apply to every business organization.

we could see his sales, cost of sales, and margins for each type of work. Once he had the information, it took about three *minutes* for him to abandon the new house-wiring business. Wiring houses is attractive business at first look. It generates a lot of sales and surprisingly good cash flow. However, it's a competitive market, which meant that there was little opportunity to improve on the 5 percent gross margins he had been earning. He chose to concentrate his resources on new commercial construction and service work.

We chose to put our initial effort into improving margins on service work. His company does a lot of service calls every week, which meant we could test incremental changes without a lot of risk and measure our results across many small, representative transactions rather than one or two large ones.

We recorded the two main components of variable costs—material and labor—which were 33.2 percent and 34.2 percent of sales, respectively. We didn't really know if those were good or bad numbers but we thought he could do better. We chose to work on improving labor costs as a percent of sales. He reasoned that, based on last year's service sales of $750,000, each percentage point of improvement would add $7,500 to the bottom line.

The dollar-per-hour cost of an electrician is what it is; there is little opportunity in his competitive labor market to reduce wages. The same is largely true for parts. They cost what they cost. Contractor $ realized that the way to improve margins was to get more work done by the same number of technicians in the same amount of time—his specific goal was to do one more job per truck per day—which brings us to the clever idea. He reasoned that technicians wasted a lot of time looking for tools and parts in their disorganized trucks. Rather than chew out the techs and punish them, he created a contest.

At every regular Friday morning meeting, he presents each service truck team a list of parts and tools used on most jobs. He tells the teams to retrieve the parts and tools from their trucks. The first team back receives $100. The idea is that they have to be organized to win the prize and that organization carries over to service calls. (He has since standardized the layout of every truck in his fleet.)

The results were remarkable. As of this writing, not only did labor decline from 34.2 percent to 26.5 percent of sales, but also his parts declined from 33.2 percent to 31.9 percent.[40] Together the improvements total 9 percent, which is astounding. For the first quarter alone, the improvements account for about $27,000 of additional margins on $300,000 of service sales. That's almost as much as he earned on $2.8 million of sales over the entire last year.

Example 2: How to Build Houses for Free

I have a lot of respect for spec-home builders. Spec-home builders put large amounts of capital, usually borrowed, on the line to build homes they believe (hope?) will sell quickly. Some of them do and some of them don't. Builders have to confront weather, subcontractors' schedules, code-enforcement inspectors, the whims of the market, and misunderstandings with home buyers who seldom seem to have heard what the builder said. They live with stress for the six months to a year that it takes to build a house and then hope it sells before interest reduces margins to zero. It's a tough business, and when they get it right, builders ought to be rewarded for their efforts.

I've asked a lot of builders about their gross margins. I most often hear estimates of between 15 percent and 25 percent. However, when we dive in and begin to separate their variable and fixed costs, their margins almost always work out to be around 10 percent or less—sometimes much less. That's because a lot of builders classify interest, land cost, closing costs, and sales commissions as overhead when they are actually variable costs. Moving them from overhead to variable costs reduces margins. That was the case with a builder I know who, after we rearranged his income statement, discovered he had a 10 percent gross profit on the 60 spec homes he built the year before we met.

---

40 We surmise that the unanticipated improvement in parts expense is because technicians didn't spend money—or time—traveling to the suppliers' stores and buying parts they already had but couldn't find on their trucks until they were organized.

That meant, of course, that for every dollar of sales, he spent 90 cents on variable costs, which left 10 cents as gross margin. His average house that year sold for $300,000, which gave him a gross profit of $30,000 per house.

$300,000 average home price x $0.10 margins
= $30,000 average gross profit per house

That's pretty simple, right? Simple, yes; satisfactory, no. He was surprised to realize how much he had to sell to break even on the cost of the many overhead expenditures normal to builders. In particular, he was struck by the realization that he had to build and sell *two* houses just to pay for his new $60,000 pickup truck!

$60,000 truck / $0.10 margin
= $600,000 sales / $300,000 house
= TWO houses!

Think about that. He, in effect, traded two brand-new houses for a pick-up truck. If that weren't enough, he was startled to realize that it took $1,000 of sales to pay for every $100 tank of gas he burned in his truck.

$100 tank of gas / $0.10 margin
= $1,000 sales to break even

I don't know which realization affected him most but affected he was.

Once the builder calculated his margins and realized their impact on breakeven, he and his team committed to finding ways to increase margins. As we've seen, there are two ways to do that. The first is to raise prices; the second is to reduce variable costs. (Of course, you could always do both!) It's difficult to simply raise prices in the housing industry because prices are capped by appraisers and comps. Therefore, the builder and his team set out first to reduce variable costs. Once they started looking, it wasn't that hard to find cost reduction opportunities. The team chose to reduce the cost of the following items:

- Build times (which affect interest and other carrying costs)

- Warranty work

- Wasted material

- Builder error

- Early sales opportunities

- Change-outs

- Feature giveaways

- Closing cost concessions

The first four items were primarily the responsibility of project managers. The company established clear timelines and budgets. They tied project managers' bonuses to their performance in all four areas and committed to supporting them and listening to their ideas. They hired an experienced quality control manager who inspected every house at least every other week to spot small problems before they become big problems. They defined standards for clean and orderly work sites that made it easy to distinguish scrap from usable material. A crew routinely picked up usable material from the scrap pile at one site and delivered it to be used at the next.

An unexpected benefit of orderly work sites was faster sales. The sales team had always insisted they could sell homes sooner if they could show unfinished homes to prospective buyers. However, they were reluctant to take prospects to chaotic work sites. Sales made earlier in the build process not only reduced interest and other costs but also gave salespeople a chance to upsell features to home buyers at the appropriate stage in the building cycle.

Upsell opportunities come and go at various stages of construction. For example, it's too late to upsell stone accents to an exterior wall if the brick veneer is already complete. The team established systems to ensure that every buyer was offered the opportunity to purchase upgrades at the appropriate time. As a result, they more than doubled sales of upgrades, such as exterior stonework, custom flooring, video and sound systems, weather packages, and patio and garage packages for cash at high margins.

The owner committed to eliminating wasteful change-outs. A *change-out* occurs when a project manager removes and replaces a completed feature. Some of the change-outs were due to lack of planning and indecision, but most of them were due to the whims of the company owner. He would walk through a partially completed home, decide that he preferred a different paint color or type of flooring, and order a change. At an average cost of $1,000 each, the company spent about $40,000 per year on needless and unplanned changes. The company established design meetings in which they selected all features in advance and well before they broke ground on a new house. They agreed to stick to the plan unless a customer paid for a change, and most importantly, the owner agreed to stop ordering random change-outs.

The company put the brakes on feature giveaways and closing cost concessions. Both were the result of habit and insecure salespeople who routinely began negotiations with concessions. They would throw in a fence or window treatment or agree to pay closing costs before negotiations even began. The company reduced such concessions in large part by making the sales team justify their concessions in sales meetings.

Although they began with cost reductions, the team did not surrender the matter of price to the appraisers and comps. They set out to raise sales prices by increasing the square footage of their homes. It's possible to carry that strategy too far by pricing a home out of the market in a neighborhood.[41] For that reason, they worked cautiously and increased square footage in small increments. On one home design, they found a way to add 50 square feet to a house for a cost of $800. At the market rate of $140 per square foot, 50 additional square feet added $7,000 to the appraised value for a potential $6,200 to gross profit.

---

41 Even if the price per square foot is in the market, the total price of a house may be too high for a particular neighborhood. Builders always have to consider both the square foot price *and* the total cost of the house.

$$50 \text{ sq. ft x } \$140 \text{ price per sq. ft}$$
$$= \$7,000 \text{ increase in value - } \$800 \text{ cost}$$
$$= \$6,200 \text{ new gross profit}$$

Once again, it's the little things that make a big difference. The 50 square feet added about 2 percent to the size and price of the home but *over 20 percent to the potential gross profit!*

$$\$6,200 \text{ new gross profit / } \$30,000 \text{ original gross profit}$$
$$= 20.6\% \text{ increase}$$

That is a big deal, and even if the market balked at paying the higher total price, the team still had an extra $7,000 of negotiating room acquired at a cost of $800.

Through all that hard work, planning, and diligent attention to detail, the company increased its margins from 10 percent to 13 percent. That may not look like much but it resulted in an increase of $9,000 gross profit per house.

$$3\% \text{ higher margin x } \$300,000 \text{ average price home}$$
$$= \$9,000 \text{ increase per home}$$

Had it applied to the prior years' sales, the 3 percent increase would have added $540,000 to the company's gross profit. At the old 10 percent margins, the company would have had to build and sell 18 homes to generate $540,000 of gross profit.

$$60 \text{ homes x } \$9,000 \text{ increase}$$
$$= \$540,000 \text{ total increase on 60 homes}$$

$$\$540,000 \text{ / } \$30,000 \text{ average margin (before improved processes)}$$
$$= 18 \text{ homes}$$

And *that* is how you build houses for free. It's not easy, but which would you rather do: Finance, build, and sell 18 homes or improve your gross profit margins from 10 percent to 13 percent? How about doing both?

Example 3: Tough Pricing Decisions

For Robert Bauman, 18 months of hard work were at risk, not to mention the future of his company. Bauman, the cabinet manufacturer we met in chapter 11, had achieved his first goal, which was to remove himself from day-to-day operations.

Over the months it took to achieve his goal, he made significant changes. He cut the hours he spent dealing with day-to-day problems from 50 per week to fewer than 10. He developed good books and used his reclaimed time to plan for growth. Among other things, he established a cash reserve to fund planned increases in inventory and accounts receivable. He developed and implemented the processes necessary to scale up production. He improved the company culture along with the quality of his team and he hired a top-notch salesperson. Perhaps, most exciting, he identified specific target markets, wrote out persona profiles, and developed a unique, value-driven offer to appeal to each one. He implemented a thoughtful inbound marketing strategy to attract customers: A new website, weekly blogs, regular podcasts, and free resources. It was working.

Everything was great except for one thing: His facility was running at full capacity. To meet his projected sales, he would need three times more space than he had.

With things running smoothly, he set to work considering his options. He spent several months looking at building a new plant, and he was evaluating the purchase of a competitor when a recently vacated facility came on the market. The facility was more than three times as large as his current plant, located on an interstate highway exit only six miles from his current location, and the rent was the same as his existing facility. He jumped on the opportunity and committed to a five-year lease. Perfect!

He and his crew made the move to the new facility themselves. The move took longer and consumed more cash than anticipated, and it resulted in a drop in billing due to lost production. However, by the end of the fourth month, they were up and running at full capacity in the new plant. That's when the problem showed up.

After months of distraction, Robert turned his attention to profitability and cash flow. What he found scared him. He called to tell me his "green line" had fallen behind his "red line." His green line, as you might suspect, is total sales for the month to date and his red line is total expenses for the same period. Comparing the two is a quick way to judge performance, and the green line should always be ahead of the red line. The comparison is not as accurate as month-end financials but can identify problems early, and it had identified a big one: He was losing money. Why? What had gone wrong?

With all the changes surrounding the move, we began to suspect all sorts of reasons. Maybe the shop wasn't organized right, maybe stations were too far apart in the big building, maybe the batch sizes were wrong, maybe they were creating too much scrap or the overhead had somehow crept higher than they thought. Maybe the move was a bad idea and they had just signed a five-year lease! We were all over the place looking for answers when we finally turned our attention to the fundamentals: his numbers.

My client always had good books and had spent a large part of the last 18 months making them into great books. We could trust what his income statement showed us, and what it showed us was clear. Although there were some cost overruns due to the move, overhead was almost exactly as planned. As for variable costs, the target for direct labor costs was 25 percent of sales, and the actual labor costs at the new plant were 27 percent. Not perfect but not terrible either. Then we found the culprit: Material costs, which had been 38 percent of sales for over a year, were now at 65 percent! We had identified the problem, and it had nothing to do with the move or the new shop, which had distracted us. We looked at scrap and counted inventory to be sure the 65 percent was an accurate number. It was.

How had Robert and I missed it? He began the move with cash reserves and his sales had dropped during the move. Lower sales meant that he was collecting more cash from old accounts receivable than he was tying up in new sales. Because of the distractions, the cash available from reserves and old accounts receivable, we just hadn't noticed until money got tight and we both saw material costs were out of control.

The rising costs were due to import restrictions and an antidumping lawsuit that affected all the materials my client used. The increases had been rolling in steadily over six months but always in small increments. My client knew about them but did not realize their impact.

Our complex problem was now a simple choice. He had to get material costs down and/or raise prices. The future of the operation depended on getting material costs back to no more than 40 percent of sales. Although he continues to work on it, it quickly became clear that he could not immediately get material prices down. That left one option: Robert had to raise prices.

Raising prices in a competitive industry is nerve-racking. As we discussed above, we are reluctant to do it because we're afraid we'll lose customers. However, difficult circumstances can make for simple choices.

He raised prices to the point at which material costs were 40 percent of the sales price. His green line is now well above his red line; he is making a profit and rebuilding his cash reserves. To our knowledge, he has not lost a sale due to price. If not for good numbers, Robert might still be running around the shop rearranging machines and conveyors, pressuring the team and raising the overall anxiety level of the company. Instead, good numbers from proper bookkeeping informed a simple but tough decision that saved his company.

Example 4: Eliminate Slippage

Eli's Pool Service contracted with me during the slow winter season. Eli's does maintenance and service on swimming pools and spas from about the first of April through the end of September. The good news was that their sales for the most recent season totaled $3 million, a surprisingly high number for the small market they serve. The bad news was that their net profit was less than 1 percent of sales. Year after year, they worked very hard for puny returns and they were tired of it. They brought me in to see what they could do to improve things.

Eli's earns the bulk of its revenue by charging for the hours technicians spend on-site. The company pays its technicians an average of $20 per hour and charges customers $80 per hour. Perfection is not possible but that's the target. In this case, perfection would be to charge a customer for every hour paid to a tech. If they could do it, they'd earn margins of $60 per hour (the difference between $20 per hour wages and the $80 per hour price) times the total hours paid to technicians.

We spent our first four sessions getting their books right. They had entered all the information, but it was not arranged properly so we couldn't see their actual margins. Once we had accurate accounting, I noticed labor costs were more than 65 percent of *labor* sales. That was a glaring problem. If they charged customers for every hour they paid technicians, their labor cost would be 25 percent of labor sales ($20 per hour labor cost / $80 revenue per hour). Charging for any fewer than 100 percent of paid hours is "slippage." It's reasonable to expect some slippage, but it was obvious Eli's fell far short of billing for 100 percent of paid technician hours.

The first step was to count the total hours paid to technicians the prior season and to divide that number by the total hours billed to customers for the same period. The answer was a dismal 32 percent! The company billed only 32 percent of the total hours it paid technicians. We had identified the problem. We named the ratio of paid hours to billed hours the "labor conversion rate" and set out to improve it. We will see in chapter 21 how Eli used the labor conversion rate first to define and measure problems and second to identify specific actions to improve productivity.

Using Margins to Price Products, Services, and Bids

So far, we have been talking about using margins to establish breakeven sales targets and to identify activities to improve margins and profitability. There is another common use for margins—to set prices for products, services, and bids. There are two important things to consider when using margins to set prices: Confusion between markup and margin pricing and confusion between cost and price. We have to get these right or we can mess up royally.

Markup versus Margin

In the third example, I said Robert used his material costs to raise prices to the point at which those costs would represent 40 percent of sales. I didn't say how he did it, which presents a great opportunity to show the important difference between using markup or margin to come up with price.

Like Robert, most of us use cost to establish price. First, we estimate the cost of a product or job then we work some calculations to come up with a price that will give us a target gross profit margin. As we will see, that's not the ideal approach but it is at least rational. Why does it seldom work out? Why do the actual margins on our income statements often fall short of our planned margins? It could be due to our employees messing up a job or to our bad cost estimates, but very often it's because our pricing never gave us a chance. To understand why, we need to know the difference between markup and margin.

Markup is an amount we add to cost to come up with selling price. *Margin* is the difference between selling price and cost. That may sound like a distinction without a difference, but the difference is very real and very important.

A markup will give you a margin, *but the margin will always be less than the markup*. For example, a 40 percent markup will result in a 28.5 percent margin. This is another of those critical subjects that may be confusing at first but is well worth understanding.

To see how it works, assume you're working to price a product or to bid a job. You've done your estimating homework and your cost for materials plus labor (your variable costs) is $1,000. You want to set your price to provide a target 40 percent gross profit margin. How do you do that?

A lot of businesses do it like this:

$1,000 cost x 40% target margin = $400

Add the two to get a price = $1,400

That is a *markup* strategy, and it will not get you to your 40 percent margin because:

$400 gross profit / $1,400 price = 28.5% margin

In the example, gross profit is $400 and total price is $1,400. The $400 margin is only 28.5 percent of $1,400. If you've been pricing your products and jobs using a markup strategy, you can see why the margins on your income statement never match your pricing plan.

In order to use a margin pricing strategy—one that will give you at least a chance to hit your target margins—you have to do things differently. The first step in pricing for margins is to express your *cost* as a percent of price. I hate that there's this confusing step in the process, but unfortunately it's there and we must live with it.

Another way of saying you want margins to be 40 percent of the price is to say that you want variable costs to be 60 percent of the price. That makes sense, right? If you want a 40 percent margin, your variable costs will be 60 percent. The simple formula for this extra step is:

1 - % target margin = % variable cost

(1 - 40% target margin = 60% variable costs)

Once you have the number (in this example, 60 percent), you can find the price that will give you a 40 percent margin.

1,000 cost / 60% variable costs = $1,667 price

The gross profit for the job is $667, which is 40 percent of the $1,667 sale price.

$$\$667 \text{ gross profit } / \$1,667 \text{ price} = 40\% \text{ margin}$$

You've done it. Your price will give you a 40 percent margin as planned. Below is a table of margin and markup equivalents.

Markup	Margin
15%	13%
20%	17%
25%	20%
50%	33%
75%	43%
100%	50%

That said, I want to be sure I haven't misled you. I have been talking about using cost to determine price *because that's what most of us do.* However, cost has little to do with purely optimal pricing decisions, which are simple: *Charge as much as the customer will pay but not less than variable cost.* That sentence captures the essence of the so-called value pricing you may have heard about. When it comes to charging customers all they will pay—in other words, charging them for what they perceive to be the value of your product or service—cost does not determine price.

To illustrate the disconnect between cost and price, imagine you found a diamond in the street. Would you sell it for pennies just because your acquisition cost was low? Or suppose your employees messed up and you had to rework an entire job. Would you expect your client to pay double? Of course not. As for variable costs, if you sell for *less* than variable costs, you will lose more money making a sale than not making it. If you charge *more* than variable costs, you may not break even on total expenses but at least you will earn a margin to help pay overhead and profit. Don't sell below variable costs, but beyond that, price and cost are only related through competition[42] and the courage you need to ask for a higher price.

How Much Does It Cost? Burdening, Cost Absorption, and Other Tomfoolery

"How much does it cost?" Such a simple question—at least it is if you have a receipt in your bag from the store where you bought "it."

We've been talking a lot about cost up to this point, in particular about the cost of variable and fixed expenses. We've seen how important it is to have accurate numbers and to keep the two types of expenses separate in order to find breakeven. Getting cost right is even more important when we use cost to establish our prices.

It seems that identifying costs should be easy, and for many types of businesses, it is. If you own a clothing store and sell dresses, it's easy to look at a bill from your supplier to see how much a dress costs. As we saw above, you can divide the cost of the dress by 60 percent to price it at a 40 percent margin. However, for those of us who provide services, bid jobs, or price manufactured products, cost can be one of the most confounding issues in business.

My experience has shown that many of us are confused about the difference between cost and price. You may ask, "How can that be?" Everyone knows that cost is what you pay for "it" and price is what you sell "it" for. It sounds simple, but there is often a lot of confusion about the "what you paid for it" part. When we want to know what something cost, we look at what we paid for it or add up all the expenses that went into producing it. Confusion sets in when we allocate a portion of overhead to individual products or services in an effort to find what people often describe as "true cost." The idea behind true cost is that every product or service consumes some part of overhead and that amount has to be added to cost. The prac-

---

42 Competition doesn't need to control your pricing if you give customers reasons, other than price, to choose your offer. But that's a topic for a separate book.

tice of allocating overhead to individual products and service is known as "burdening" or "cost absorption" and it leads to all sorts of confusion and bad decisions. *Burdening is a completely arbitrary and therefore meaningless exercise*—or would be meaningless except that it can do great harm.[43]

You may not recognize the terms *burdening* or *cost absorption* but I'll bet you've encountered the concepts. Think back to a conversation you had about cost. If it's been a while, ask a colleague how much it costs, for example, to run a machine out in the plant. I doubt you will get a receipt-in-the-bag straight answer. More likely, your friend will lean back in his chair, tent his fingers, take a deep breath, and lay out the logic behind the number he is about to give you: "When we take into account the cost of capital tied up in the machine, plus wear and tear amortized over its expected life, plus maintenance, and the cost of power, tools, and the operator's wages and our square-foot charge to recover building rent and, of course, adding in something for profit...I figure it costs $XXX dollars per hour to run that machine."

Say what?

Rather than unravel that complicated answer, let's look at the answer I received from Mr. Benson, the owner of Benco, the west Texas manufacturing operation we met in chapter 10. His company manufactures products and also does job-shop work on a bid basis. Customers request quotes for rebuilding or modifying machines and for building custom machines. This bid work is an important part of their business and accounts for 45 percent of their revenues.

In a conversation about pricing bids, I asked Mr. Benson about his labor costs. He told me his labor "cost" was $80 per hour. I had been in the Benco parking lot many times and had seen the cars parked there. I doubted that

---

43 I am not alone in thinking that burdening does harm. James Womack and Daniel Jones in their book, *Lean Thinking*, credit the turnaround success of a Japanese manufacturer to the elimination of burdening. The company created a new system "in which only a small fraction of costs was allocated [to products] from overhead so it was possible to know if product families were producing an adequate [gross] profit." Without the change, no one would "have known which products were making money and which were dragging the firm down."

any of the employees made $80 per hour, which is roughly $160,000 per year. I modified my question and asked Mr. Benson about the *actual* cost of labor, the out-of-pocket costs for which they wrote checks, including hourly wages, insurance, other benefits, and payroll taxes. *That* total was $25 per hour. So where did $80 come from? In order, as he put it, "to make something to cover overhead," management added an overhead charge of $55 to each labor hour as "burden." No one could tell me the origin of the $55 number, but there it was, embedded in what everyone in the company acknowledged as a labor "cost" of $80 per hour.

To be clear, there is nothing wrong with selling $25 labor for $80 but the $80 figure is a *price*, not a *cost*. The problem at the company was that the $80 figure quickly became actual cost in their minds, replacing the real variable cost of $25 per hour. That led to bad decisions. The company not only lost work due to overpricing bids but also routinely passed on work paying less than $80 per hour *because they thought they would lose money.* I hope you recognize what's wrong with that logic. A job that pays $75 per hour would contribute a $50-per-hour margin ($75 price - $25 cost = $50 margin) toward paying overhead and profit.

The problem with their logic was that the company confused cost information—the $25-out-of-pocket, receipt-in-the-bag, I-wrote-a-check-for-it, actual labor cost—with a pricing decision, the $55 burden. They added $55 to cost to create a margin, which is price. But Benco didn't call it price; they called it cost. It's crazy. Their idea of true cost wasn't true cost at all. It was a random number created out of thin air. It was a combination of variable costs and a number attributed to "overhead" arbitrarily thrown together and meaningless. It's so convoluted that it's been hard to even write about it.

I've seen enough of this to make an informed guess as to why people do it. It's because they want to be sure to set prices high enough to recover overhead. It's as if increasing the so-called cost of products or services through burdening will somehow trick or remind them to charge enough to recover their overhead. If everyone at Benco thinks an hour of labor actually costs $80, they are not likely to sell it for $20 per hour, which would generate an actual loss. But *neither are they likely to sell it for $75* which, as we've seen, would generate a nice margin.

The confusion about using cost for pricing decisions originates with confusion about the behaviors of variable and fixed costs. As we have discussed at length, variable costs go up and down with sales. Fixed costs, or overhead expenses, are independent of sales. They remain the same, or very nearly so, from month to month. If we win a sale, we incur additional variable costs. If we lose a sale, we avoid those additional variable costs, but in either case, our overhead costs remain the same. Variable costs, then, are the *costs of the product or service*. Overhead is the *cost of maintaining the capacity to produce* the product or service. It is meaningless to divvy up overhead and arbitrarily assign it to individual products or services.

"Okay," you're thinking, "I get it. Variable costs are the true cost of a product but I still have to pay overhead.[44] Don't I have to add those costs to the cost of my products in order to recover all my costs?" The answer is, *"No. No. No."* Adding one cost to another does nothing at all to recover costs. Overhead costs *are not* product costs and should be kept separate. We have spent the last 20 or so pages discussing the advantages of *separating* variable and overhead costs. Burdening just recombines them in a subjective manner and messes everything up.

So how do we recover overhead costs if we don't add them to the cost of our products and services? We sell enough to recover overhead through margins, the difference between the selling price and variable costs. If, after calculating breakeven, we determine that we need higher margins, the answer is not to increase our burden rate. It is to increase our margins by raising prices or lowering variable costs, or both. We don't need an alloca-

---

44 Sometimes a portion of overhead expenses is due entirely to a particular product or service—for example, when a building and some dedicated equipment are used to make only one product. In that case, it is reasonable to insist that the product should "pay" all the overhead costs associated with the building and equipment. However, the fact that the product is made with dedicated resources does *not increase the cost of the product* or create a need to burden them. Instead, the situation calls for a breakeven target for the product that will generate enough margin to pay all of the dedicated overhead plus an additional amount for net profit.

tion of overhead to do any of those things. Once the overhead is paid, our margins become profit. Where burdening creates confusion about cost and leads to bad decisions, *margins lead to clear thinking, clear targets, and rational decisions.*

When you use the breakeven techniques we've been discussing, you calculate how much you *have to sell* to break even or to make a budgeted gross profit. That is a target. When you burden your products or services with overhead, you have, consciously or not, predetermined what you *will sell.* That is an assumption. Big difference. The first number is useful; the second one is not. In fact, although they base critical pricing decisions on presumptions, most people who burden, such as Mr. Benson, couldn't tell you the assumptions on which they based their decisions. If they can, the answer will include the sort of convoluted, specious reasoning our hypothetical colleague used to explain his machine costs.

Burdening would be a wasteful but benign exercise except for the confusion it creates and the fact that it renders all the breakeven tools we discussed above useless. Burdened variable costs are not really variable costs because they include some fixed costs. Fixed costs are not really fixed costs because a portion of them has been allocated to variable costs. Without accurate variable and fixed costs, you can't know your true margins, and without true margins, you can't find your breakeven, determine the effects of price increases or discounts, set efficiency targets, or use any of the other tools that margins and breakeven make possible. *Understanding cost does not have to involve the confounding topic of burden. Separate your variable and overhead costs and keep them separate.*

How to Increase Your Margins

We could keep going with stories about how people use margins and breakeven to make better decisions and more money. How are *you* going to increase *your* margins? You're not likely to boost margins and become suddenly wealthy from a big contract, a competitor's demise, or an unexpected economic upswing. Therefore, you must do it with discipline. As we saw in the examples above, you do it by paying attention. You do it with small, incremental gains in a lot of areas. You do it by controlling freight costs, credit card charges, sales commissions, inventory levels, discounts, price decisions, marketing, scheduling, and better marketing. You do it by setting targets for labor costs as a percentage of sales, measuring improvements, making your team aware of them, holding them accountable, and providing incentives for hitting them. You do it by finding a way to sell one more hour of service each week. You do it by adopting lean management techniques. All of us can improve margins once we realize the importance of small changes.

Every business decision has a cost or target, and every cost or target has a breakeven. You can become a "walking breakeven calculator" who can make informed decisions quickly on virtually any business question by knowing the most important number in your business operations: your margins.

Take the following steps to apply margins and breakeven to your business:

1. Separate your variable and fixed costs.

2. Calculate your margins as a percentage of sales.

3. Determine a target gross profit margin (total overhead expenses, total overhead plus a target net profit, total overhead plus debt service, pay for a salesperson, etc.).

4. Divide your target gross profit amount by margins to find the breakeven sales required to hit your target.

5. Set KPIs to improve your margins and track your progress.

6. Use a margin, not a markup, strategy when setting prices.

7. Be sure you are using real, not burdened, cost when using cost to price products, services, or bids.

If that sounds tedious, get a good accountant to do it for you. Your job is not to compile numbers but to use the information to make better business decisions.

The 1% Rule Explained

The 1% rule says that a 1 percent increase in gross profit (for example from 40 percent of sales to 41 percent of sales) for small business will increase net profits by 14.5 percent. How does that work?

The average small business[45] in the US earns a net profit of 7 percent of sales (actually 6.9 percent). A profitable business, by definition, is operating above breakeven which means that any increase in margins will increase net profit by the same amount. For the average small business, a 1 percent increase in margin will increase net profit from 7 percent to 8 percent, which is a 14.5 percent improvement.

If you don't remember anything else from this book, remember the 1% rule. It clearly shows the power of small changes. Everybody, *absolutely everybody*, can improve margins by 1 percent. Here's how it works for a strategy of reducing variable costs. Can you think of another way to improve your margins by 1 percent? (Hint: Raise your prices 1 percent.)

Before 1% Increase in Margins			After 1% Increase in Margins		
		% of Sales			*% of Sales*
Income	1,000,000	100%	Income	1,000,000	100%
Variable Costs	600,000	60%	Variable Costs	590,000	59%
Gross Profit	400,000	40%	Gross Profit	410,000	41%
Fixed Costs	330,000		Fixed Costs	330,000	
Net Profit	$70,000	7%	Net Profit	$80,000	8%

An $80,000 profit is 14.5 percent more than the $70,000 profit.

---

45 Large businesses generally earn less net profit as a percentage of sales. Walmart, for example, had sales of $514 billion in 2018 and net profits of $3.8 billion, for less than 1 percent of sales as net profit. In 2018, its best year by far, Amazon earned $10 billion on sales of $233 billion, a 4.3 percent of sales net profit.

CHAPTER 15

Using the Balance Sheet

To fully understand where we want to go, it helps to have an accurate assessment of our exact starting point.

—Peter Diamandis and Steven Kotler,

coauthors of *Abundance: The Future Is Better than You Think*

We've all heard the word *audit*, which we associate negatively with the IRS. The word is derived from the Latin word *auditus,* which means "hearing." Many kings were illiterate, at least with regard to financial reports, so they had their accounts read out loud to them in an audit. A courtier simply spoke aloud what the king owned and owed. Most of us don't have courtiers so we must rely on a balance sheet which, in the simplest terms, is just a list of information.

Using the Balance Sheet to Simplify Your Life

My client, Jeff, is a contractor and he's among the lucky ones. He's lucky not because he's a contractor, or because he won a lottery or because his dad started the business and taught him the ropes (which he didn't). Like many of us, he started his company from scratch using sweat equity and his own capital. He shouldered the risk and built a company with virtually no understanding of three of the four disciplines of business.

No, Jeff isn't lucky because of a head start. He's lucky because his personality and natural behaviors align with the attributes of a successful business owner. Jeff is organized, not because anyone told him to be but because he cannot stand to be unorganized. He makes decisions quickly, not because he read a book about decision-making but because he can't stand to leave decisions hanging. He does not tolerate mediocre employees or shoddy work because, in his words, "Why would I?" He visits his job sites unannounced and knows what's going on in his business because he naturally *has* to know. Jeff does not agonize, equivocate, rationalize, or regret. His business, and profits and cash flow, show the effects of good leadership and management. He works hard but he makes it look simple.

I mention Jeff because his need to know led him to value accurate accounting. We spent several months getting his books set up in QuickBooks and developing systems to be sure they are always current and properly compiled. Jeff had been using his books almost exclusively to track margins and profitability through his income statement when one day I saw him writing numbers on a pad of paper. His desk was covered with documents, including vendor bills, timesheets, customer invoices, and a written list of the inventory in his shop. He also had his credit card and bank account apps open on his computer.

"What are you doing?" I asked.

"I'm just trying to figure out where I stand," he answered. I asked him what he meant. "I've got cash in the bank and more coming from receivables but I have outstanding checks, payables, and payroll taxes due. I have to finish buying material for sold jobs but I already have a lot of it. I'm just trying to figure out where it all balances out. I gotta figure out where I stand." It was a perfect opportunity to demonstrate one of the most practical uses for the balance sheet.

Jeff wasn't in the habit of looking at his balance sheet. I know he had seen it because we had gone over it together. However, my explanations and demonstrations didn't sink in then because I was giving him answers to questions he hadn't asked. Now he was asking, "Where do I stand?"

"Are your books current?" I asked. "Are all of your checks, invoices, bills, and credit card charges entered?"

"Yes." Jeff takes his books seriously and makes entries every day.

"Great. Click REPORTS and print an accrual-basis balance sheet dated as of today."

He did.

"Look at your total current assets and subtract your total current liabilities," I said. "Current assets are things that are likely to provide cash pretty quickly, and the current liabilities are those that are likely to require cash pretty quickly. The difference between the two is a measure of where you stand from the perspective of cash demand. All those things you've been tracking in your head are right there in the report. That's what it's for."

Jeff printed his balance sheet and in a few seconds, he had his answer, which looked great. The balance sheet showed he had more than twice the amount of current assets as current liabilities.

Who among us has not suffered through the mental exercise of trying to keep track of where we stand? Many of us do it every day. We think to ourselves, "I have this much cash, so-and-so should pay by Friday, but if he doesn't, I can put my supplier off until next week, but damn, I forgot about the payroll deposit that's coming out, and the bank's calling about the payment due on my line of credit…" and so on and on. Maybe you struggle through the exercise while driving, which is distracting and probably as dangerous as texting. With a proper balance sheet, you can put (most of) those mental gymnastics to rest by simply looking at the report.

In chapter 11, I said the balance sheet is, at its core, a list. It shows what we own, what we owe, and what's left over. The balance sheet is the scorecard, a compilation of information that shows the cumulative effects of every transaction from the day the business began to the date of the report. That is, of course, assuming we have kept proper books from day one.

Preparation

Before you begin working with your balance sheet, you need to quickly ensure that: a) the balance sheet is part of a set of reports all covering the same period, b) it was prepared on the accrual basis, and c) it balances.

What follows is the balance sheet that goes with Small Co. LLC's income statement. I say "goes with" because the three financial reports—the income statement, balance sheet, and statement of cash flows (which we'll see next)—come in sets. A set is a group of statements created at the same time and covering the same period. You know that this balance sheet belongs with the Small Co.'s income statement not only because of the name and dates at the top of the report but more importantly because of the number next to "current earnings" toward the bottom of the balance sheet. The number—in this case, a nice even $100,000—should exactly equal the net profit on the corresponding income statement from above. It does. (You can look back or take my word for it.)

If the numbers didn't match, it would be a sign of something wrong. That usually happens when reports cover different periods or were prepared at different times (and when somebody posted a few bookkeeping entries in the interim). If the numbers didn't match, you would have to insist that your bookkeeper correct them before going any further.

As we will see, the three reports provide complementary and supplementary information. Therefore, it's important that they cover the same period. If that sounds complicated, don't worry about it. Just make sure that the number next to "current earnings" on your balance sheet exactly matches the number next to net profit on your income statement before you put a lot of effort into analyzing your numbers.

Next, check to see that the report was prepared on the accrual basis. In QuickBooks, reports are marked "accrual basis" or "cash basis," usually in the upper left-hand corner of the report. If it's not apparent by looking at your report, ask the person who prepared it.

Finally, you have to be sure that the balance sheet balances. On Small Co.'s balance sheet below, the number next to total assets ($1,270,000) should be exactly equal to the number next to total liabilities plus equity, which for Small Co. is also $1,270,000. Although it's very rare and I don't know how it happens, I have seen computer software produce a balance sheet that didn't balance. If that's the case, there's something fundamentally wrong and you need a competent bookkeeper or CPA to fix it.

Little Co LLC
Balance Sheet
As of Dec. 31, 20xx

Accrual Basis

ASSETS

Short-term Assets

Cash in bank	$100,000
Accounts receivable	$120,000
Inventory	$150,000
Total Short-term Assets	$370,000

Long-term Assets

Trucks	$150,000
Equipment	$300,000
Building and land	$750,000
Accumulated depreciation	$(300,000)
Net Long-term assets	$900,000
TOTAL ASSETS	**$1,270,000**

LIABILITIES

Liabilities

Short-term Liabilities

Accounts Payable	$125,000
Credit Cards	$50,000
Total Short-term Liabilities	$175,000

Long-term Liabilities

Loan on Truck	$100,000
Mortgage: Land and building	$550,000
Operating Loan	$100,000
Total Long-Term Liabilities	$750,000
TOTAL LIABILITIES	**$925,000**

EQUITY

Paid-in Capital	$25,000
Owner Contributions	$70,000
Owner Withdrawals	$(750,000)
Cumulative Earnings (retained earnings)	$900,000
Current Earnings	$100,000
TOTAL EQUITY	**$345,000**
TOTAL LIABILITIES AND EQUITY	**$1,270,000**

Your bookkeeper or accountant has provided you with an accrual-basis balance sheet that balances. You've verified that it's part of a set of reports covering the period you're interested in. Now what?

We said earlier that the income statement was a tactical document you use frequently throughout the month and year to guide operational decisions. The balance sheet is a more strategic document that tells you where you stand and where you ought to stand to preserve and improve the financial condition of your company. There are two ways to use the information on a balance sheet:

1. The first use is as a simple **list** of account balances. Account balances provide a lot of useful information but by themselves provide only limited insights for determining or improving the financial condition of a company.

2. The second use is to calculate ratios among items listed on the balance sheet. Ratios provide insight into the financial condition of a company and what you can do to improve it.

List Information

The first use of a balance sheet is as a list and scorecard. Subject to the subtleties we discussed in chapter 11, the balance sheet is simply a list of numbers that shows us the way things were at the time the report was produced. Every number next to every account on the balance sheet is the current balance, or score, for that account. It's a tally of all the transactions that affected the account from the inception of the business up to and including the day and hour of the report.

In the case of a bank account, the current balance is the result of deposits and withdrawals. Small Co.'s bank balance may have varied over the years from overdrawn to millions of dollars and back to hundreds of dollars on December 31 when the balance was $100,000. Every account has followed a similar journey to arrive at its current balance.

As we saw with our plumber in chapter 1, it would be impossible to create or understand account balances without proper books. We also saw that without them, we would find ourselves lost and stressed.

As we begin to look at the report, recall from chapter 11 that accounts are organized on the balance sheet according to "liquidity." In other words, assets are ranked by how quickly we can convert them to cash and liabilities by how quickly we will need cash to pay for them.

Little Co LLC
Balance Sheet (Part 1)
As of Dec. 31, 20xx

Accrual Basis

ASSETS

Short-term Assets	
Cash in bank	$100,000
Accounts receivable	$120,000
Inventory	$150,000
Total Short-term Assets	$370,000

Cash: $100,000

Cash is the first account we notice on the balance sheet. That's understandable because we're all interested in cash. We look for it first because cash is the most liquid of all accounts. After all, cash *is* cash.

Accounts Receivable: $120,000

The next thing we will see on most balance sheets is accounts receivable, the total of what customers owe us from sales. We all know what our customers and clients owe us, right? Not "kind of" or a "ballpark" estimate of what they owe us but rather the actual amount due. If we keep proper books, we do because our balance sheets will show us what is due, net of partial payments, deposits, credits, discounts, late charges, and any other transaction that affects accounts receivable. We don't have to remember because all the information is there at a glance, contained in a balance as of a particular day. There's not another good source for this information, not your memory and not a legal pad with scribbles on it. Neither comes close to accounts receivable recorded in proper books that are kept up-to-date.

A special note about accounts receivable: if you invoice your customers through specialty software, it's important to set up procedures so that the specialty software reports current billing information accurately, directly, and routinely to your accounting software.

Inventory: $150,000

After accounts receivable comes inventory. Ahhhh, inventory. In this case, Small Co. shows that it owns $150,000 of inventory. Inventory is an asset. It comprises goods, materials, or parts that we own until we either sell them outright or include them as part of a sale, such as when an electrician uses parts and materials to wire a building. It's also possible that we expense inventory as obsolete or as scrap after we run over it and poke a hole in it with a forklift. As soon as we sell it, use it, or expense it, inventory becomes a cost of goods sold or scrap expense and is no longer an asset.

My experience has shown that retailers, distributors, and manufacturers are generally familiar with inventory and all of its difficulties. They are used to seeing a hefty number next to inventory on their balance sheets and reconciling their actual inventory with what's shown on their books. In contrast, contractors, tradespeople, and service industries don't often show inventory on their books, in spite of the fact that their shops and trucks are overflowing with extra parts and materials purchased and paid for over the months and years. The parts and materials are not listed as assets because they expensed them as cost of goods sold when they bought them.

If you expense inventory the day it arrives, yet still have it on hand devouring your cash and cluttering aisles in the shop, well, that's a distortion. Your balance sheet is incorrect and your income statement overstates expenses and understates profit.

Inventory is a confounding, difficult, and special source of trouble for small businesses. It's hard to keep track of inventory, but it's impossible to know how much *or even if* you earned a profit unless you know how much inventory you own. That's a real problem because every decision you make using the income statement relies on an accurate picture of margins and profit, which depends on cost of goods sold, which depends on how you handle inventory.

I'm flogging the inventory horse because the vast majority of contractors, people working in the trades, service tech companies, and small manufacturers do not keep an accurate count of inventory, which means they cannot produce an accurate income statement or balance sheet.

Inventory Surprise

Kevin, the electrical contractor we met earlier, is a good case in point. Kevin had been in business for almost two years when we met. He and his helper worked out of his truck because he didn't have an office or shop space. Over our first year working together, he tripled sales and added two trucks to his fleet, each of which was manned by a journeyman and apprentice electrician. He also leased an office and shop, which meant that he acquired both a shop and two more trucks in which to accumulate "stuff."

At the very beginning, we set up proper books, which his wife kept well and diligently. We calculated target margins and labor and material costs for every job. We reviewed the jobs and books every month but were disappointed because the results never seemed to materialize as planned. We looked at all sorts of reasons, but his high cost of materials as a percent of sales made it apparent that inventory was a big part of the problem. I'd seen parts and material accumulating in the shop but had no idea what they were worth. I exhorted, cajoled, and pleaded with Kevin to count the inventory in the shop and on his trucks. He was always too busy. Finally, he and his wife agreed to meet me at his shop on Labor Day. Before we started, we placed an over/under bet for the value of inventory on hand. I bet on the over.

It took a day to count inventory in the shop and several days to count the inventory in his trucks. It took another week to put a value on the totals, but the result was a big win for me. Kevin was shocked. The inventory was more than four times his guess. We made bookkeeping entries[46] to reduce his expenses by the amount of inventory he had on hand, which more than doubled his profit for the year. I could give you plenty of similar examples.

If you don't have inventory, count yourselves among the lucky few, but before you do, be sure that you *really don't* have inventory. If you do have inventory, there are three ways to handle it in your accounting.

The first method is not to handle it. Expense everything you buy the moment you buy it and live with incorrect financial reports.

The second method is to keep perpetual inventory, which is the fully proper way to account for inventory. With perpetual inventory, you add items to inventory when you buy them and remove items when you sell them. Between purchase and sale, you always know what items you have in stock, plus or minus inevitable mistakes. This is the accurate and proper way to keep inventory, but it's a lot of work and most of us won't do it.

Fortunately for most of us, there's a third method—a compromise—for handling inventory. The compromise method is to expense inventory when it arrives and then count what remains at the end of each month. Give the numbers to your accountant, who will adjust the cost of goods sold and inventory accounts. This way, your financials will be right once per month, which is pretty good.

Total Current Assets: $370,000

The total current assets figure is the sum of cash, accounts receivable, and inventory. Your company may have other short-term assets, such as money due to you from a loan to a key employee. In any case, the total current assets represent the total assets you can likely convert to cash quickly. This is the first half of the information Jeff was looking for when he was trying to find out where his finances stood.

---

46 He had expensed his inventory as cost of goods sold when he received it. The bookkeeping entries we made increased his inventory assets and reduced his cost of goods sold expense. The result was that profit for the year increased by the amount of the adjustment.

Little Co LLC
Balance Sheet (Part 2)
As of Dec. 31, 20xx

ASSETS

Long-term Assets

Trucks	$150,000
Equipment	$300,000
Building and land	$750,000
Accumulated depreciation	$(300,000)
Net Long-term assets	$900,000
TOTAL ASSETS	**$1,270,000**

Next in line are long-term assets. These are assets that are more difficult to convert to cash and generally subject to depreciation, which means that we cannot expense the entire cost of the asset in one accounting period.[47] Long-term assets are arranged in order of liquidity. With Small Co., trucks come before equipment, which comes before building and land. The presumption is that the owner could sell a truck more quickly than specialized equipment, which the owner could sell more quickly than the building and land. None of that may be true in reality but those are the presumptions.

All the long-term assets are recorded on the books at cost, or what the company paid for them. They may be worth less, as is probably true of Small Co.'s trucks, or they may be worth more, as is possible for the company's building and land.

Accumulated Depreciation: ($300,000)

Accumulated depreciation is an estimate of how much your long-term assets have worn out since you purchased them, or more precisely, it's an estimate of how much the law and your tax decisions allow you to claim they have worn out.

---

47 What may or may not be depreciated, or written off as an expense, is subject to complex tax laws that require interpretation by qualified CPAs. Regardless of how they are treated for depreciation and tax purposes, most assets that are useful well beyond a year should be recorded as long-term assets.

Total Assets: $1,270,000

The total assets figure is the sum of all the listed assets. On Small Co.'s report, total assets are $1,270,000. This is the number that will have to balance with total liabilities plus total equity.

Liabilities

Liabilities come next on the balance sheet. Recall that liabilities are debts the business owes to nonowners. It is money due to people and entities, such as vendors, credit card companies, and banks. It's very important to know what you owe and it's critically important to know what you must pay soon. For that reason, liabilities are also recorded in order of liquidity which, in contrast to assets, is a measure of how quickly you'll need cash to stay current on your debt obligations.

Little Co LLC
Balance Sheet (Part 3)
As of Dec. 31, 20xx

LIABILITIES AND EQUITY

Liabilities	
Short-term Liabilities	
Accounts Payable	$125,000
Credit Cards	$50,000
Total Short-term Liabilities	$175,000

Current Liabilities: $175,000

Small Co.'s current liabilities include $125,000 of accounts payable to vendors and $50,000 of debt to credit card companies. The current liabilities for Jeff's company is the second half of the information he needed to understand "how it all balances out." As with current assets, most business owners keep a ballpark running total of what they owe in their heads, but again, ballpark estimates and memory are soft ground upon which to build a company.

Long-Term Liabilities: $750,000

Long-term liabilities are debt obligations that we are not required to pay off entirely in the current accounting year. At Small Co., long-term debt includes $100,000 remaining on truck loans, $550,000 remaining on land and building loans, and another $100,000 outstanding on an operating loan. In proper books, the amount of debt shown on the balance sheet is the current balance due as of the date of the balance sheet.

Little Co LLC
Balance Sheet (Part 4)
As of Dec. 31, 20xx

LIABILITIES

Liabilities	
Long-term Liabilities	
Loan on Truck	$100,000
Mortgage: Land and building	$550,000
Operating Loan	$100,000
Total Long-Term Liabilities	$750,000
TOTAL LIABILITIES	**$925,000**

Total Liabilities: $925,000

The total liabilities figure is the sum of current and long-term liabilities. For Small Co., total liabilities of $345,000 represent what the company owes to outsiders. We will add this number to total equity to see if our balance sheet balances.

Equity

Equity[48] is the last and probably least understood section in the balance sheet. It's not as complicated as it is unfamiliar. People don't often use it, and accountants sometimes make entries into equity accounts for obscure reasons

---

48 In some corporate structures, these accounts are critically important. They can determine how profits must be distributed and whether or not the owners can deduct business losses on their tax returns.

most of us don't understand. In theory, equity is what would be left over for the owners if all assets were sold and all obligations were paid. In reality, it's an estimate of that amount, because as we've discussed, assets are usually worth more or less than what's shown on the balance sheet. (Liabilities, on the other hand, are usually dead-on accurate. That's because we're not going to offer more to settle debt and our creditors are not likely to accept less.)

Little Co LLC
Balance Sheet (Part 5)
As of Dec. 31, 20xx

EQUITY

Paid-in Capital	$25,000
Owner Contributions	$70,000
Owner Withdrawals	$(750,000)
Cumulative Earnings (retained earnings)	$900,000
Current Earnings	$100,000
TOTAL EQUITY	**$345,000**
TOTAL LIABILITIES AND EQUITY	**$1,270,000**

Paid-in Capital: $25,000

The first line under equity on Small Co.'s balance sheet is "paid-in capital." It shows that the owner(s) originally paid $25,000 into the company at start-up.

Owner Contributions: $70,000

The Owner Contributions line shows that the owners have paid an additional $70,000 into the business.

Owner Withdrawals Total: ($750,000)

The owner withdrawals figure is the total amount the owners have taken out of the company as draws or dividends (money taken as a share of profit rather than salary or payroll). Most of the business owners I work with are surprised at the amount of money they take out of their businesses over time. Consider Allison, the owner of the cleaning company we met in chapter 12 who discovered how much money she took as draws. She was shocked and there's a good chance you will be too.

I need to emphasize that the owner withdrawals account shows the total of draws taken since the company began. It is *not* what was taken this year. We can find the amount we took in the current year on the statement of cash flows. The three combined Small Co. accounts—paid-in capital, owner contributions, and owner withdrawals—tell us that Small Co.'s owners contributed a total of $95,000 to the business ($25,000 + $70,000) and took out a total of $750,000 as draws.

Cumulative Earnings (sometimes called "retained earnings"): $900,000

The next account under the equity section is "cumulative earnings." This is a really interesting number that represents total company net profits from the beginning of the company *to the end of the last fiscal year*. It does not include profits for the current year, which are listed next under the appropriately titled account "current earnings." At the beginning of each new fiscal year, bookkeepers or software add current earnings to cumulative earnings and reset current earnings to zero. The *cumulative* earning account for Small Co. LLC shows the company has earned $900,000 from the day it began business *through the last day of the prior fiscal year*.

Current Earnings: $100,000

The *current* earnings account shows the company earned $100,000 this calendar year. Together, the current and cumulative earnings accounts show that the company has earned a total of $1,000,000 since it began business ($900,000 cumulative earnings + $100,000 current earnings). That helps explain how owners who contributed a total of $95,000 to a company were able to withdraw $750,000.

Total Equity: $345,000

Total equity is the sum of the numbers listed above it in the equity section of the balance sheet. For Small Co. LLC, the total equity is a positive $345,000. It's possible for a company to have a negative, or "deficit," equity. That happens when the company suffered losses or the owners took out more in draws than the combined total of profits and contributions. Whether positive or negative, total equity is the book value of the company and represents what would be left over for the owners if all assets were sold and all liabilities were paid the amounts shown in the books. As we discussed in chapter 11, the company is almost certainly worth more or less than book value. We will see in chapter 19 how sellers and buyers arrive at an actual value for a company.

Balancing the Balance Sheet: $1,270,000

The total assets on Small Co.'s balance sheet are $1,270,000, and the sum of liabilities and equity is $1,270,000, so Small Co.'s owners know their balance sheet balances and all's right with the world (well, at least this part of it).

Ratios: A Way to Compare

As Hans Rosling, the statistician and author, said, "The most important thing you can do to avoid misjudging a thing's importance is to avoid lonely numbers. Never, ever leave a number by itself. If you are offered one number, always ask for at least one more. Something to compare it to."

In other words, lists are useful but they are made up of lonely numbers. By using ratios, we are able to make useful comparisons.

Lonely numbers don't tell us much about the financial health of a company. To show you what I mean, suppose you look at a balance sheet and notice that a company has $1 million cash in a local bank. A $1,000,000 cash balance would look pretty good to most of us but that fact doesn't tell the whole story. Suppose you look farther down the report and see the company owes $1,500,000 to suppliers and credit card companies. Things look entirely different now. As we would say in financial terms, the company has a "0.67 to 1 quick ratio," which tells us the company has 67 cents cash available to pay each $1.00 of current debt ($1,000,000 / $1,500,000 = 0.67).

You don't need to know a whole lot about finance to understand that the company with a 0.67:1 current ratio is in a precarious cash position. The company is going to have to hustle to collect receivables, make some cash sales, sell some assets, or borrow money in order to meet its debt obligations.

Most of the information about the health of a company is found in similar ratios.

Ratios are information expressed as X divided by Y, or something per something. Ratios produced from a balance sheet are a principal source of insight into the financial health of a company. They can also tell us how well a company manages accounts receivable (days sales outstanding), how well it manages inventory (inventory turns), and how likely it is to make debt payments on time (debt coverage ratio).

The list of possible ratios is almost endless, but below are nine that you should know and understand for your business. They will give you an idea about the health of your company, a current score, and a way to track and measure improvement. Again, *you* are not going to calculate the ratios. We'll leave that to the accountants.[49]

I've grouped the ratios into three categories: liquidity, efficiency, and profitability ratios.

Liquidity ratios:

1. Current ratio
2. Quick ratio
3. Cash ratio
4. Debt coverage ratio

Efficiency ratios:

1. Days sales outstanding
2. Inventory turns

Profitability ratios:

1. Gross profit margins
2. Net profit margins
3. Debt coverage ratio

---

49 If you really want to do the calculations yourself, the wonderful world of financial ratios is well described on websites such as https://corporatefinanceinstitute.com/resources/ knowledge/finance/financial-ratios/.

You might be thinking, "Yeah, right, I'm supposed to have enough cash on hand at all times to pay all my monthly bills? Get serious. Nobody does that." Yes, they do, and the ones who do lead different lives than those who don't. But in any case, that's not what I'm suggesting. I am suggesting that you keep *three times that amount* on hand! (See chapter 18.) Three times your average monthly overhead *plus* three times your monthly debt service payments as cash in your bank, at a minimum. You should pursue that goal like a duck pursues a June bug. It will change your life.

Debt Coverage Ratio

$$\text{DEBT COVERAGE RATIO} =$$
$$(\text{NET EARNINGS} + \text{DEPRECIATION} + \text{INTEREST}) / \text{TOTAL DEBT PAYMENTS}$$

All debt is repaid from net profits. The fact that debt is repaid from profit is one of the three main reasons that businesses make money but don't have any. I have had countless discussions with business owners who earn a net profit, spend all their cash repaying debt, and then wonder why they don't have any money. Regardless of your short-term cash position, *you must earn enough gross profit to cover all your overhead plus the principal due on your debts.* The debt coverage ratio[50] tells you how well you are doing in that regard. The debt coverage ratio uses information from the income statement rather than the balance sheet.

The ratio compares net earnings for a period to the debt payments due in the same period. (Recall that you add depreciation to net profit because it's a noncash expense that reduces profit without consuming cash. You add back interest expense because it's already included in your total debt payments.)

---

50 Although some of the information is available on the balance sheet, the debt coverage ratio uses information from the income statement. I put it in this section because this is where we are discussing ratios. The debt coverage ratio also requires us to know our total debt payments due each month, which is not shown directly on any financial statement. Finding total debt payments is a matter of adding up all your scheduled monthly payments. For this example, let's say Small Co.'s annual numbers (all fictional) are: interest $40,000, depreciation $30,000, and total payments made to long-term debt over the year are $100,000, which equal $2,830 per month—trucks; $3,629 per month—mortgage; and $1,874 per month—operating loan.

Liquidity Ratios

Liquidity ratios measure your ability to pay *near-term* debt payments on time. Near-term is another way to say "most worried about" and usually applies to payments due within 90 days. Liquidity ratios focus on short-term assets and liabilities because liquidity is about cash flowing in and out of your business primarily as a result of income and expenses. The ratio compares short-term assets that will provide cash to short-term liabilities that consume cash. This is the information Jeff, the contractor we met earlier, was trying to keep track of in his head. There are four really useful liquidity ratios:

Current Ratio

The current ratio compares *all* your current assets, including inventory, to your current liabilities. It's a measure of your ability to pay all your short-term debt obligations, assuming you could convert all your current assets to cash in time to meet your obligations.

Small Co. LLC's current ratio:

$$
\begin{array}{ll}
& \$370,000 \quad \text{current assets} \\
/ & \underline{\$175,000 \quad \text{current liabilities}} \\
= & \$2.11{:}\$1.00 \quad \text{current ratio}
\end{array}
$$

The ratio tells Small Co. managers that they have $2.11 of current assets for every $1.00 of current debt. This is a pretty healthy ratio.

Quick Ratio

QUICK RATIO = (CURRENT ASSETS - INVENTORY) / CURRENT LIABILITIES

The quick ratio is similar to the current ratio but measures your ability to meet your short-term obligations with current assets, excluding inventory. The quick ratio excludes inventory because you usually can't get your money out of inventory as quickly as cash and receivables. It may be optimistic to assume you can collect your receivables in time to pay your bills but at least they are one step closer to cash than unsold inventory.

Small Co. debt coverage ratio:

	$100,000	net profit
+	$30,000	depreciation
+	$40,000	interest
=	$170,000	adjusted net profit

	$170,000	adjusted net profit
/	$100,000	total debt payments
=	$1.70:$1.00	debt coverage ratio

The debt coverage ratio shows that Small Co. LLC is earning $1.70 for each $1.00 it is paying back on debt.

Efficiency Ratios

We may not use the term but we are all familiar with efficiency ratios. One that comes immediately to mind is "miles per gallon." Suppose you're talking to a used car salesman who tells you a car is really efficient, saying, "It gets 30 miles!" That statement is meaningless, but we are so conditioned to ratios that most of us would unthinkingly fill in the missing "per gallon." We are familiar with lots of other efficiency ratios: Dollars per hour, bushels per acre, cents per pound, gigabytes per second. They are all useful because they provide different information than a Hans Rosling lonely number. "Miles" means something completely different than "miles per gallon." The same is true of business ratios.

In business, we use efficiency ratios to measure how effective we are at converting resources into sales, profit, and cash, which tells us how well we're progressing through the cycle of business. Improving efficiency is the key to making more money, increasing available cash, dominating the competition, and reducing stress load. There are two especially useful efficiency ratios to measure, monitor, and improve cash and operational efficiency: days sales outstanding and inventory turns.

Days sales outstanding = (accounts receivable / annual revenue) x 365

Accounts receivable devour cash. You've made it all the way through the business cycle from assets to profit but get hung up on the last step: Converting profits into cash. That's because your customers have your money. The "days sales outstanding" ratio tells you how long, on average, your customers keep your money.

Inventory turns = Cost of Goods Sold / Average Inventory on Hand

Inventory is another major cash consumer. You can't pay your bills with inventory sitting at your store, in the warehouse, on trucks, or at the shop. Inventory turns measure how much inventory you require to generate a dollar of sales. The more times you "turn" your inventory, the less cash you will have tied in it. For example, a company with $1,000,000 of annual cost of goods sold and an average of $500,000 of inventory on hand "turns" its inventory twice per year ($1 million sales / $500,000 inventory = 2 turns). If the company could manage the same sales and cost of goods sold with an average of $250,000 of inventory, it would turn its inventory four times per year and liberate $250,000 of cash.

Profitability Ratios

Gross profit margin = gross profit / total sales

Yes, this is the same gross profit margin I described in chapter 14 as the most important number in business operations. It's the number you use to determine breakeven and to make all the operating decisions we discussed earlier. Because it represents gross profit *per* sales dollar, it's a ratio too.

Net profit margin = net profit / total sales

Net profit is the bottom line on your income statement. Dividing net profit by sales tells you how much of your sales dollar survived both variable and fixed costs to reach the bottom line. (For the average small business in the United States, this number is 6.9 percent.)

$$\text{RETURN ON ASSETS = NET INCOME / TOTAL ASSETS}$$

Return on assets tells you how effective you are at using your assets to generate profit.

What Should It Be?

When clients see their ratios for the first time, they always ask, "What should it be?" That's a great question, and the short answer is "better." Even if you have twice the cash necessary to pay short-term debt, more would be better; even if you turn your inventory 10 times per year, 11 times would be better; and even if you have 60 percent gross profit margins and 20 percent net profit margins, 61 percent and 21 percent would be better. The benefit of knowing your ratios is that you understand "better," have a target to shoot for, and a way to measure your progress.

More specific answers to the question "What should it be?" depend on your industry. There are normal ratios for virtually every industry. For any particular industry, there are ranges of ratios that reflect the differences between high and low performers and large and small companies, and among companies in different geographical regions. Books containing ratios are available in libraries, through industry associations, and through organizations such as the Risk Management Association. They are all interesting reading either as printed publications or online. However, the easiest way is to consult your bank.

When you apply to a bank for a business loan, someone sits in a back room calculating ratios from the financial statements you provided. The bank will use the information (along with your credit score, collateral, and their assessment of your personal character) to decide whether to lend money to you. With regard to ratios, (good) banks have the information and experience to determine which ratios sing out "Behold!" and which ratios cry out "Beware!" They know which ratios indicate a company will thrive and which indicate trouble ahead. You need to know too. Although it may not always seem like it, banks are your allies in this regard. You and your bank have a common interest: You both want your business to survive and thrive.

They want you to survive so you can pay them back and to thrive so they can lend you more money in the future. You want to survive and thrive because, well…because it's your business.

Ask your banker which ratios they use to assess the health of your business, and ask them to provide the industry standard ratios for comparable companies in your area. If they won't give you the information, find a different bank.

Using Ratios to Plan: How Much Money Do I Need to Fund a Planned Increase in Sales?

Recall the blistered business owner in chapter 7 who sold fixtures to builders. He had opened a new business in July, and by the time we talked in February, he was selling more than $100,000 of merchandise per month. He did it after starting his business with only $30,000 cash. It was a big success story, except for the fact that both he and his company were on the verge of collapse.

When he opened his business, he concentrated on sales. He understood pricing and margins and made a nice profit but he was out of cash. He had accumulated inventory but more than half of his business was special orders. That meant he had to buy even more inventory than what he had in the warehouse. His suppliers had him on-and-off credit hold due to inconsistent payment history and his customers were mad at him. He was up against competitors who allowed 60- to 90-day credit terms and he felt compelled to match their terms.

His problem was that merchandise cost him 60 cents of each sales dollar, which meant that for every dollar his sales increased from one month to the next, he needed another 60 cents of cash to finance the cost of the sale. The more he sold, the worse his problem became.

By the time he called me, he had $140,000 of stagnant inventory, $250,000 in accounts receivable, $10,000 of cash, and about $140,000 in past due bills. That means he had $400,000 worth of current assets to offset $140,000 of past due bills. His current ratio was $2.85:$1.00, which is good.

$$
\begin{array}{rll}
 & \$140{,}000 & \text{current asset} \\
+ & \$250{,}000 & \text{current asset} \\
+ & \$10{,}000 & \text{current asset} \\
/ & \$140{,}000 & \text{current liabilities} \\
\hline
= & \$2.85{:}\$1.00 & \text{current ratio}
\end{array}
$$

However, his cash ratio was a miserable $0.07:$1.00.

$$
\begin{array}{rll}
 & \$10{,}000 & \text{cash} \\
/ & \$140{,}000 & \text{current liabilities} \\
\hline
= & \$0.07{:}\$1.00 &
\end{array}
$$

Although he had plenty of inventory and accounts receivable to cover his debt, he only had 7 cents cash available to pay each dollar of near-term debt. It didn't have to be that way. He could have avoided a crisis with proper financing and a disciplined sales strategy—in other words, with planning.

I happen to know someone—that would be *me*—who went back to school at age 40 to get an MBA degree.[51] I had worked for almost 20 years in commodities and wanted to know if it were possible to know the future (which would be a very useful skill). I discovered that it is not, but neither are we condemned to stumble into oblivion. We can't *know* the future but we can *influence* it through informed decisions and planning.

The benefit of planning is, of course, that if you understand what is likely to happen, you can do something about it. We all know that, so why do so few of us plan for the effects of sales on our cash? The first reason is that it doesn't occur to us. I've attended countless gatherings of small business owners, and I don't recall ever hearing a discussion about forecasting the cash required to fund increased sales. If I hear a conversation about cash, it's usually to bemoan a current cash crisis.

The second reason is that most of us don't think about the negative consequences of sales. Sales are good! Sales mean we are doing things right.

---

51 I said in the introduction that I have had no formal training in bookkeeping or accounting. It's true. In 54 hours of graduate level business courses, I never heard a mention of bookkeeping or breakeven.

Sales mean we have customers and they like our offering. Sales mean money flowing (eventually) into the business. Sales mean margins and profit. If we have an opportunity to make a sale, most of us are going to take it. What could be bad about increasing our sales? Well, we've just seen what could be bad about increasing sales.

The third reason is that most of us don't know how to plan future cash requirements. We'll see how it's done using ratios shortly. More important than *how*, we'll see that it *can* be done. Again, if you love numbers, you may enjoy the details. If not, skip to the section titled "Putting It All Together" to see what you can learn, then have your accountant do the forecasting.

We are going to forecast the cash requirements by making "working capital" calculations (there are other ways to forecast as well). You may not use the term but you deal with working capital every day. It's the money that cycles in and out of your business through current assets and liabilities. In financial terms, working capital is the difference between current assets and current liabilities.

The three things about increased sales that most affect working capital are increases in accounts receivable, inventory, and accounts payable.

Increases in accounts receivable and inventory consume cash. Increases in accounts payable provide cash. (If you have positive margins, don't have inventory, and don't sell to customers on credit, go for it! Ramp up your sales. You are off the working capital hook!) Working capital calculations forecast the negative effects of increasing receivables and inventory and compare them to the positive effects of increasing accounts payable.

To see how it works, let's assume our fixture salesman sells $1,000,000 of product per year and that the cost of the goods he sells is 60 percent of sales. Assume that 100 percent of his sales are made on account, that it takes 60 days to collect receivables and that he keeps three months' supply of inventory on hand. We'll also assume that his suppliers require him to pay in 30 days. To forecast the amount of required working capital, he would calculate the effects of accounts receivable, inventory, and accounts payable like this:

The Negative Effects of Accounts Receivable on Working Capital

The working capital required to fund accounts receivable is the number of days accounts receivable are outstanding times the average credit sales per day (in our example, 100 percent of sales are credit sales). For example:

$$
\begin{array}{rll}
 & 60 & \text{days outstanding} \\
\times & \$2{,}740 & \text{average sales per day} \\
\hline
= & \$164{,}400 & \text{cash to fund receivables}
\end{array}
$$

The result tells us that his accounts receivable tied up an average of $164,400 of working capital to support $1,000,000 in sales.

The working capital required as a percent of sales:

$$\$164{,}400 \ / \ \$1{,}000{,}000 = 16.44\%$$

This means that for each $100 of sales, his business needed $16.44 of working capital to finance accounts receivable.

The Negative Effects of Inventory on Working Capital

The working capital required to fund inventory is equivalent to the average number of days inventory is held times the cost of average daily sales:

$$
\begin{array}{rll}
 & 90 & \text{days on hand} \\
\times & \$2{,}740 & \text{average sales} \\
\times & 60\% & \text{cost of sales} \\
\hline
= & \$147{,}960 & \text{cash to fund inventory}
\end{array}
$$

The result tells us that his inventory tied up an average of $147,960 of working capital to support $1,000,000 in sales.

To find the effect of inventory on working capital as a percent of sales, divide it by total sales to get a percentage:

$$\$147,960 / \ 1,000,000 = 14.8\%$$

This means that for every $100 increase in sales, he needed an additional $14.80 to finance inventory.

The Positive Effects of Accounts Payable on Working Capital

The working capital *provided* by accounts payable (which are loans to us from our suppliers) is equivalent to the number of days they allow us to pay times the average daily *cost* of sales:

	30	days credit allowed
x	$1,644	cost of average day's sales
=	$49,230	of working capital provided by accounts payable

That tells us his suppliers provided him with $49,230 of working capital under their terms. (In fact, he had $140,000 borrowed from suppliers because he was behind in his payments.) Converting that number to a percentage of sales shows that:

$$\$49,230 \ / \ \$1,000,000 = 4.92\%$$

This means that for each $100 increase in sales, we can expect our suppliers to provide us with $4.92 of financing.

Putting It All Together

Using these numbers, we'll see that, had he known in advance how much money he needed, the fixture salesman would have known his $30,000 savings weren't enough and he could have done things differently and survived.

Under the conditions he allowed, the net effects of accounts receivable, inventory, and accounts payable on the working capital required to support $1 million of sales are:

	$164,400	to fund receivables
+	$147,960	to fund inventory
-	($49,230)	provided by suppliers
=	**$263,130**	**total working capital required**

The poor guy was doomed from the start. He just didn't know it.

What could he have done differently? He could have limited customer terms to 30 days, managed inventory at a 30-day supply, and negotiated 60-day payment terms with his suppliers. Had he done all that, his working capital *requirements would have dropped from $263,130 to $33,880* and he would likely still be in business today.

	30	days outstanding
x	$2,740	average sales per day
=	$82,200	cash to fund receivables

	30	days on hand
x	$2,740	average sales
· x	60%	cost of sales
=	$49,320	cash to fund receivables

	60	days credit allowed
x	$1,644	cost of average day's sales
=	$98,640	

The totals look like this:

	$82,200	to fund receivables
+	$49,320	to fund inventory
-	($98,640)	provided by suppliers
=	**$32,880**	**total working capital required**

He would have protested that it's tough to limit customers to 30-day terms, to get 60-day terms from suppliers, and to sell from limited inventory but people are surprised at what they can do when they have to!

Better terms are only part of what he could have done. He also could have paced his sales to match his available capital, and he could have approached a bank to get financing *before* the crisis. Bankers love business owners who approach them ahead of a crisis and who demonstrate an understanding of their cash requirements. You should be aware, however, that there is a risk that your banker will faint when you provide him or her a working capital analysis based on your current, proper, accrual-basis, double-entry books.

If you use an accountant to help you with the calculations (as you should), he or she is likely to provide a result as a percentage of sales, as we calculated above for Small Co. Percentages are a useful way to report working capital requirements because they allow you to plan for any level of increased sales. For example, you could say that you need $263,130 to fund $1 million in sales, or you could say you need working capital equal to 26.40 percent of sales. You can use that number to find working capital requirement for any amount of sales without having to go through all the calculations each time.

In case you were wondering, the only reasons the fixture salesman survived as long as he did were: (a) he had not yet reached the $1 million sales mark (he was only beginning to sell at that annual rate when I met him), (b) he wasn't paying his suppliers on time, and (c) he had borrowed money from friends, family, and the SBA.

The list of potential uses for the information on your balance sheet far exceeds what we've looked at so far. However, it is worth knowing that you're not likely to get a bank loan, sell your business, or know if you made a profit without a proper balance sheet.

Next comes the statement of cash flows. It is the most confusing financial statement but the easiest one to use!

CHAPTER 16

Using the Statement of Cash Flows

Most important is cash… Without this, business can hardly be carried on.

—LUCA PACIOLI, VENICE, 1494

I HAVE SAID REPEATEDLY THAT THE STATEMENT OF CASH FLOWS IS THE MOST confusing and least understood of the three financial statements and it is. But it's also the easiest to use. That's because you aren't going to use it to find margins and breakeven, to analyze the effects of price changes, or to calculate a bunch of ratios. You are just going to look at it and see what it tells you.

We saw in chapter 12 that if your income statement shows you made money but you don't have any, there are only three possible reasons (four when you consider embezzlement, but we'll get to that later).

You may have less cash than profit because of one or a combination of these reasons:

1. You haven't been paid yet.

2. You already spent the money paying off debt or buying assets.

3. You took the money as distributions.

Sometimes things work in your favor. You might wind up with more cash than profit because:

1. You collected more than you sold.

2. You borrowed more than you repaid.

3. You sold more assets than you bought.

4. You put more money into the business than you took out.

5. You have depreciation expense on your income statement.

Your cash balance will almost always be a mix of those factors. How in the heck are you supposed to keep track of all the possible combinations of cash-consuming and cash-providing activities? The answer is the statement of cash flows. Look at it and it will tell you exactly where your cash went over any selected period, which is the first step toward managing that precious resource.

Preparation

Unlike the income statement and the balance sheet, you do not need to check to see that the statement of cash flows was prepared on the accrual basis because you cannot produce the report on a cash-basis. You do need to make sure that it's part of a set of three financial statements prepared at the same time and covering the same period.

Below is the statement of cash flows for Small Co. You can see that it goes with the previously shown income statement because of the dates on the reports and because the net profit of $100,000 (line 3 on the statement of cash flows) is the same as net income on the income statement. You can see it goes with the balance sheet because of the dates and because the "cash in bank" on line 20 of the balance sheet is $100,000, exactly the same as the ending cash balance on the statement of cash flows.

The statement of cash flows, like the income statement, is a period report. It tells you what happened to your cash between two specific dates—in Small Co.'s case, between January 1 and December 31 of a particular year.

We saw in chapter 12 that the report groups information into three categories:

1. Changes due to operating activities are changes in cash that result directly from your efforts to make sales. Think of changes due to operating activities as changes that originate with sales and expenses on the income statement. Operating activities affect current assets, such as cash, accounts receivable, and inventory, and current liabilities, such as accounts payable and credit card debt.

2. Changes due to investing activities are changes to cash that result from buying or selling long-term assets, such as trucks, equipment, and real estate. Investing activities might also include the purchase or sale of intangible assets, such as stocks or bonds, or your acquisition of a competitor's company.

3. Changes due to financing activities are changes due to borrowing or repaying long-term debt and to contributions and withdrawals made by the owners.

We saw from their balance sheet that Small Co. is in a cash flow bind. They only have $100,000 of cash to pay $175,000 of current liabilities. The owners are undoubtedly thinking, "What the heck? We had $150,000 at the beginning of the year and we made $100,000 profit, so why don't we have enough cash to pay our bills?" Their statement of cash flows looks like this:

Small Co. LLC
Statement of Cash Flows
January 1, 20XX through December 31, 20XX

1	**BEGINNING CASH BALANCE**	**$175,000**
2	**CHANGES DUE TO OPERATIONS**	
3	Net profit for the period	$100,000
4	Accounts Receivable (A/R)	($75,000)
5	Accounts Payable (A/P)	$20,000
6	Credit cards	$5,000
7	Inventory	($30,000)
8	Depreciation	$30,000
9	**Net change due to operations**	**$50,000**
10	**CHANGES DUE TO INVESTMENTS**	
11	Truck: F-250 Diesel original cost	($75,000)
12	**Net change due to investment**	**($75,000)**
13	**CHANGES DUE TO FINANCING**	
14	Note on F-250 diesel	$50,000
15	Changes to operating note	($35,000)
16	Changes to real estate mortgage	($40,000)
17	Owner's net withdrawals and contributions	($25,000)
18	**Net change due to financing**	**($50,000)**
19	**Net cash increase/decrease for the period**	**($75,000)**
20	**CASH AT END OF PERIOD**	**$100,000**

Small Co. had $175,000 in the bank on January 1 (line 1) and made $100,000 profit[1] (line 3). So why don't they have $275,000 cash instead of $100,000 (line 20) at the end of the year? The precise answers lie in all those plus and minus numbers listed between the beginning and ending cash balances. Small Co. management can see immediately that:

---

1 From the Small Co. LLC income statement above.

1. Accounts receivable (line 4) used $75,000 of cash. (Reason 1: They haven't been paid yet. The amount owed to them by customers increased by $75,000.)

2. They invested in a truck (line 11), which used $75,000 of cash. (Reason 2: They spent cash buying assets.)

3. Inventory (line 7) increased, which consumed $30,000 of cash. (Reason 2: They spent cash buying assets.)

4. They repaid parts of their operating and real estate loans (lines 15 and 16), which consumed $75,000 of cash. (Reason 2: They spent cash repaying debt.)

5. The owners took $25,000 (line 17) out of the company as distributions. (Reason 4: They took cash.)

That's a total of $280,000 of cash *consumed* by the various activities. Fortunately for Small Co., the report shows they also had activities that provided cash:

1. The company made a profit (line 3) of $100,000.

2. Their accounts payable and credit card debt (lines 5 and 6) increased, which provided $25,000 cash. (Reason 5: They borrowed more from suppliers and credit card companies than they repaid to them.)

3. They had $30,000 of depreciation (line 8). (Reason 8: Depreciation is an expense that reduced profit but did not require cash.)

4. They borrowed $50,000 (line 14) to help offset the cost of the new truck. (Reason 5: They borrowed more toward the purchase of the truck than they repaid.)

Those activities *provided* a total of $205,000 cash. The difference between cash provided (came in) and consumed (went out) over the year was:

$$\$205,000 \text{ cash provided} - \$280,000 \text{ cash consumed}$$
$$= (\$75,000) \text{ net cash consumed}$$

The net effect of all those activities was a decrease in cash of $75,000 (line 19), which explains exactly why cash dropped from $175,000 (line 1) at the beginning of the year to $100,000 (line 20) at the end of the year.

If you owned Small Co., how could you use this information? The simple answer is to reduce the negative numbers and increase the positive numbers. A more specific answer is to look at each line and take action, beginning with the biggest negative numbers:

- **Accounts receivable.** You could calculate your days outstanding ratio for accounts receivable and then measure, manage, and hold people accountable for increasing cash sales and speeding collection of accounts receivable.

- **Inventory.** You could calculate your inventory turns ratio and concentrate on measuring, managing, and holding people accountable for increasing inventory turns.

- **Truck purchase.** You could borrow the full value of the truck (assuming it's not too late) in order to recover all or part of the $25,000 of cash down payment. (The truck cost $75,000, with only $50,000 borrowed, so $25,000 down payment came from cash.)

- **Draws.** You could put back the $25,000 cash you took as draws. (see "Cash: The Universal Cure for What Ails You" in chapter 18).

- **Loans.** Perhaps you could combine your operating loan and real estate loans into a long-term real estate note with lower annual payments.

These are just a few ideas of what you could do. Of course, the best idea is to understand your cash position throughout the year and to manage receivables, inventory, asset purchases, and all your other activities as you go along.

Most of the careless moves that wipe out cash happen because people are unaware of their current position and the effects of their actions. It is doubtful that Small Co. management would have put $25,000 down on the truck (or even purchased it) or taken $25,000 in draws if they understood that they would have a $75,000 cash shortfall by year-end. They might even have improved their collections and been more disciplined in buying inventory before they hit a cash crisis. Remember, what gets measured gets better.

Before we move on, and if you're not confused enough, the statement of cash flows for your company will likely have many more entries than Small Co.'s. There will be items such as payroll taxes due, amortization, sale of long-term assets, prepaid expenses, notes due to shareholders, and all sorts of other pluses and minuses. It can be enough for you to swear off the statement of cash flows entirely but please don't. The report is far too valuable to abandon just because you don't fully understand it.

Use the shortcut you learned in chapter 12. Look at the report and find the big numbers first. The activities next to negative numbers consume cash. If you don't understand why, ask your accountant and then take action to reduce them. Activities next to positive numbers provide cash. Again, if you don't know why, ask and then take action to increase them.

Congratulations, you've made it through the tough part. You've learned why and how bookkeeping and financial reports help you make better decisions and more money. You've seen how to reduce your stress load and all the suffering that comes with it by ensuring your proper books contain current and accurate information. As we will see next, you do that by having an outside accountant close your books each month.

CHAPTER 17

Closing Your Books

Knowing is the last 10 percent between you and an elegant solution.

—Nat Greene, *Stop Guessing:*
The 9 Behaviors of Great Problem Solvers

I've been telling stories throughout this book involving other people and their companies. It's time to tell a story about me.

One of the companies I helped start manufactures heavy duty rock-grinding equipment. These are 350 to 700 horsepower machines like the big yellow ones you see at construction sites.[2] I was across town in the manufacturing plant one afternoon when a customer called me. A planetary gear box on his machine failed, and he was out of business until he could get a replacement. I was already at the plant so instead of asking someone else to do it, I took the matter into my own hands. I boxed up a new $23,000 planetary drive, strapped it onto a pallet, and arranged overnight delivery with a trucking company. I felt pretty good about myself as I called the customer back to tell him his part was on the way. He was pleased to know he would be up and running the next day.

Three months later, I was in Texas and stopped by one of the customer's

---

2 These are really cool machines (check them out at www.ironwolf.com).

jobs. I asked how the machine was running and how the job was going. He said things were going well, *but*...he had a problem.

"I would sure appreciate prompt billing," he said.

"What do you mean?" I asked.

"Well, I ordered a planetary drive for this machine over three months ago, and I haven't been billed for it. I don't even know what it cost. Bills that come in months after the fact make it really hard to plan."

Ohhh nooo! is what I thought, but what I said was, "That's inexcusable. I will get to the bottom of it as soon as I get back to the office."

I didn't tell him that I was the billing department at the company and I was the one who failed to send him an invoice. I went back to my office after shipping the part and it never crossed my mind again until he brought it up. My mistake could have cost us $23,000 (and a customer), which is no trifling amount. I often wonder how many other mistakes went unnoticed and how much they cost us.

Maybe you've made a few expensive mistakes:

- Have you ever forgotten to invoice a customer? (How do you know?)

- Has a supplier ever billed you for someone else's purchases? (How do you know?)

- Have you ever double-paid an invoice because you pay from statements rather than invoices? (How do you know, and did your supplier issue a credit, or do they keep poor books too?)

- Have you ever had suspicious charges show up on your credit card or bank statement? (How do you know?)

- Have you ever looked at your bank balance and thought it can't be right? (Why? What tipped you off and what did you do about it?)

- Have you ever had a customer call to dispute the balance they owe you? (How did you resolve the issue?)

Even if you're diligent about keeping current, proper books, there will be mistakes and omissions. There will also be disputes with customers, vendors, and maybe your bank or the IRS. If you hope to defend yourself in disputes, you must have processes that enable you to find mistakes and omissions. You can't rely on luck or a customer reminding you like I did. The first and most important defense is to close your books each month.

Closing your books is a two-step process. The first step is to make sure all your invoices to customers and bills from suppliers for the month have been entered in your books. The second step is to have an *outside accountant,* by which I mean *not* an employee reconcile your balance sheet every month (you will see why it should not be an employee in chapter 20).

Most of us, when we think of reconciling, think of reconciling with our banks, but that's just the beginning. Closing your books means that an outside accountant reconciles *every single account on your balance sheet and they do it every month.* "To reconcile" means to match and agree, and in order to do that, you have to have something to match and agree *with.* Your accountant will reconcile some of your accounts with separate entities such as banks or credit card companies. They will also reconcile other accounts, such as inventory, with your internal bookkeeping records.

To see how reconciliation works and why it matters, consider the following current assets:

Cash: If you keep actual cash in your business, your accountant will have to reconcile your cash box with your internal records. They will start with the beginning cash on hand from last month's balance sheet, add cash you put into the box, and subtract all the expense receipts that explain why cash was taken out of it to find the current balance. What's that you say? You don't have expense receipts to account for cash? Well, then where did it go? Who took it? How will you justify cash expenses to the IRS in an audit?

Bank balances: Your accountant will use statements provided by your bank to reconcile the balance on your books with the balance on your bank's books. Reconciling with banks is the foundational, bare-minimum, absolutely-no-excuse-for-not-doing-it check on your bookkeeping. If for no other reason (and there are plenty of other reasons), someone had better do it before you sign your tax return.

You know that amount you've been "off" with the bank? Your accountant must find and fix that. Now.

Accounts receivable: Your accountant might reconcile your accounts receivable with your customers' records but they usually don't. That's because your customers don't send you statements showing how much they owe you. That means your accountant will reconcile your accounts receivable with your internal records. They will compare who owed you what at the end of last month against who owes you what at the end of this month. The differences have to reconcile with new charges and customer payments.

Even if they don't have good books, most small businesses have some sort of software for invoicing customers, and that software produces an "aged accounts receivable" report. That's the report that shows who owes you how much and spreads the amounts across the sheet in columns titled "current," "1–30 days past due," "31–60 days past due," and so on.

It never fails that when we open the aged accounts receivable report for the first time, new clients blurt out, "That's not right!" followed by, "So-and-so already paid, this guy owes more than that, and how come that guy's balance is negative?" The only thing we know for certain is that the report is wrong. Your accountant will reconcile your accounts receivable using last month's closed report as the beginning balance. New credit sales add to the balance, and recent payments subtract from it. The reconciled total should exactly equal the current accounts receivable balance shown on your balance sheet. No more "That's not right!" and no more issues like the one below.

Aside from knowing who owes you what by when, reconciling accounts receivable can prevent problems such as the one that cost Joe Boline at least $28,000. Joe was a neighbor who owned a media company. His company put content such as software, videos, and text on CDs, duplicated them in large quantities, and distributed them around the world.[3] It was a great business.

I was in my front yard talking to Joe when he told me he had fired his long-time office assistant that day. I asked why.

"She took $28,000 from the company," he answered.

"Wow. How did she do it?" I asked.

"She's been in charge of posting payments to accounts receivable for the past 10 years," he answered. "She created a bank account for a fake company with a name similar to my company's. Every now and then, she would get a customer's payment on account, make a deposit into her bank, and delete the receivable from our books. She never did it with big amounts, always $1,000 to $1,500."

"How did you catch her?" I asked.

"Just pure luck," he answered. "A customer called about a charge on an old bill. When I looked for it in the books, it wasn't there. I asked her about it, and I could tell something was up. It took a while but she finally admitted what she had been doing. She's been with me for over 10 years. You hear about this kind of thing, but I can't believe it happened to me. It makes me sick. We looked back over just the last six months and found she had taken at least $28,000."

"What did you do about it?"

"She doesn't have any of the money left in her account so it's no use trying to get it back. And she was a loyal employee for all those years so I just fired her."

Loyal employee for all those years? I doubt it. You will see in chapter 20 that I'm not as nice as Joe, but in any case, having an outside accountant reconcile accounts receivable could have prevented the theft.

---

3 Joe is no longer in business, but he had a good run for 15 years before the internet replaced CDs as the means to distribute digital information.

Inventory: We saw above that you cannot know if you made a profit—let alone how much—if you don't keep track of inventory. You can't catch errors and omissions either.

Reconciling inventory is a matter of matching your actual inventory on hand with what's shown in your books. Counting inventory can be a tedious process at first, but one of the advantages of reconciling inventory is that you will find ways to do it more efficiently. You will organize your store, warehouse, shop, and trucks to make it easier to count. You will create processes through which people account for the inventory they take from stock or buy at the supply house. You will have less damaged and lost inventory because it will be organized rather than scattered. You also will have better numbers with which to make decisions.[4] I could fill a book with stories about inventory that mysteriously disappears. When everyone knows you reconcile, inventory is much less likely to "walk off."

Your accountant can help set up inventory reconciliation procedures. Had I reconciled inventory at my manufacturing company, I would have caught the fact that I had not billed my Texas client for the planetary drive.

Long-term assets and depreciation: Most long-term assets reconcile against internal records. It's easier to reconcile long-term asset accounts than current assets (or liability) accounts. That's because you will have fewer monthly transactions that affect trucks, equipment, and real estate than you will transactions that affect cash, accounts receivable, and inventory. However, if you *do* buy or sell a truck, equipment, or real estate, that fact needs to show up on your balance sheet. Your accountant will also make monthly entries to reflect the appropriate depreciation adjustments for the month.

Current liabilities—accounts payable: Accounts payable are easier to reconcile than accounts receivable because your vendors and suppliers (should) provide monthly statements to reconcile with your books. Your accountant will check to see that the charges and payments shown on your

---

4 The best way to handle inventory is not to have inventory. If you think you can't do that, look into lean processes.

books match the charges and payments on the statement using the same process they use to reconcile a bank account.

This is where you discover those double payments, billed charges for items you did not receive, or charges that don't reconcile with delivery tickets. You might even discover that someone has been running their business with charges billed to your account.

Current liabilities—credit cards: Your accountant will reconcile your credit card with credit card statements the same way they reconcile your bank account. Credit cards provide an easy means for people to steal from you, especially in an era of identity theft.

Long-term liabilities—long-term debt: The payment terms of long-term debt are, or can be, set out in loan documents and amortization schedules.[5] Reconciling long-term debt is making sure that the amount of debt shown on your balance sheet matches the amount shown on your lender's records. This is a simple process if your accountant keeps up with it.

Equity: Your accountant reconciles your equity accounts against internal records. They will compare beginning account balances from last month to ending balances for this month and use internal documents to account for the changes. Incorrect entries to equity accounts can have serious tax consequences and can reveal some unsettling activities. If I had reconciled the equity accounts in one of my companies, I could have prevented a devastating issue that involved a missing $340,000 and a lot of ruined lives. I'll tell you more about it in chapter 20.

Other accounts: There will likely be more accounts on your balance sheet that those shown in the previous example, but every single one of

---

5 *Amortize* is a Latin word meaning "dead pledge." An amortization schedule shows the details of how a loan will be repaid, or "killed off." An amortization schedule shows how much of your fixed payment is repayment of principal (which affects your balance sheet) and how much of the payment is interest expense (which affects your income statement). Although the payment remains the same, the split between principal and interest changes every month. Your accountant can easily separate the two and make correct entries every month so that both your balance sheet and income statement are correct.

them can and should be reconciled against internal or external records every month.

Closing your books each month sounds like a lot of work, and it is in the beginning. But remember, you are not going to do it and neither, as we learned from Joe Boline's experience, is your in-house bookkeeper.

Here's what you need to know about closing your books:

1. Your outside accountant should do it, not you and not your bookkeeper.

2. Closing will enable you to find and correct mistakes and omissions while they are still fresh in your mind.

3. Closed books provide a starting point for next month's reconciliations. When you find mistakes or omissions in this month's books, you will have to look back only as far as last month's reconciliations for accurate beginning balances. You will not have to remember transactions from the distant past.

4. Your financial reports will be correct and contain accurate data for making informed decisions.

5. Reconciliation is your duty to every person and entity with whom you do business. (The third double of the triple-double of double-entry bookkeeping.) Your transaction partners can't reconcile their books with you if you don't reconcile your own books.

In the last section, we are going to look at more benefits of having good books, beginning with the universal cure for whatever ails you: a cash reserve.

SECTION IV

OTHER BENEFITS OF GOOD BOOKS

CHAPTER 18

Cash: The Universal Cure for Whatever Ails You

Hannibal antes portas! ("Hannibal is at the gate!")

—ANCIENT ROMAN SAYING

ANNIBAL BARCA WAS THE CARTHAGINIAN GENERAL WHO BROUGHT elephants across the Alps, defeated the Roman army at Cannae, and marched around Italy for 15 years. He was a source of dread for the Romans who lived in constant fear he would attack and conquer the city of Rome. To business owners, a shortage of cash is the equivalent of Hannibal Barca.

A large and ever-widening gap exists between business owners who have cash reserves and those who don't. Having a cash reserve is the number one predictor of a positive mindset in business owners (and likewise for most everyone else!). Cash changes everything. Business owners with cash are more relaxed, make better decisions, take advantage of opportunities, and focus on the future. Without cash, Hannibal is always at the gate.

Cash is more than just a relief to business owners. It brings with it a compound effect: Businesses with cash make more money than those without it. There are many reasons for that, including:

- Business owners with cash take 2 percent net-10 discounts. Those without cash pay 19 percent on credit card debt.

- Business owners with cash buy from suppliers who offer value. Those without cash buy from suppliers who offer credit.

- Business owners with cash hire quality people who add value to the company. Those without cash are afraid to hire anyone because of the expense.

- Business owners with cash fire the obnoxious salespeople who disrupt the company culture. Those without cash are hostage to obnoxious salespeople who bring in marginal deals.

- Business owners with cash schedule jobs according to economic priorities. Those without cash schedule jobs according to who will pay first.

- Business owners with cash fire bad clients. Those without cash tolerate bad clients because they need the sale.

- Business owners with cash earn discounts and save freight on scheduled purchases. Those without cash pay higher prices and freight on rush purchases.

- Business owners with cash bid jobs with proper margins. Those without cash bid low to get jobs and keep the cash flowing.

- Business owners with cash negotiate from a position of confidence. Those without cash negotiate from a position of desperation.

- Business owners with cash see marketing as an investment that pays returns. Those without cash see marketing as an expense to be avoided.

- Businesses owners with cash take advantage of new opportunities. Those without cash are unaware of new opportunities.

- Businesses owners with cash work "on" their businesses and plan for the future. Those without cash work "in" their businesses and are surprised by the future.

- Business owners with cash buy out their competitors at bargain prices. Those without cash sell out to end their suffering.

That's a long list of differences. I have experienced both sides of each item in the list. You can no doubt add to the list from your experience. The effects of the differences are that businesses with cash prosper from compounding benefits. Those without wither under compounding consequences. A cash reserve is an absolute imperative for a business to thrive.

To establish your reserve,[6] start by defining a reserve target. Your first target should be enough cash to pay one month's expenses *plus* one month's debt service. You can find your monthly overhead by looking at your income statement and averaging overhead expenses for the past three months.

Debt service is the amount you have to pay, on average, to stay current on your accounts payable, bank and credit card debt, and any other monthly debt payments. Debt service is not as easy to find as expenses because the amounts are not itemized on any of the three financial statements. To find your debt service, look at your liabilities on your balance sheet, and for each item listed, determine how much you pay each month to stay current. Look at vendor and credit card statements, amortization schedules, payroll tax forms, and other documents to find your average monthly payment for each item.

The next step is to open a dedicated bank account for the reserve. Open the account in a different bank than your operating accounts. Do not set up digital access to the new account. Make it hard to access the funds. The idea is to build barriers to protect your reserve and resolve against inevitable temptation to use the cash for things other than an emergency.

The third step is to fund the reserve. For most of us, cash is tight, and

---

6 Michael Michalowicz provides a complete system for managing your company by managing your cash in his book, *Profit First*. I highly recommend that you read it.

even the idea of carving out a month's reserve is daunting. The only way to do it is by paying attention to where your cash goes and imposing discipline.

The first discipline is to increase profits. Use the tools in this book to set your gross profit high enough to cover both your overhead expenses and debt service. Anything less and it will be impossible to create a reserve (or to survive).

The second discipline is to understand and get control of your cash flow. If you make a profit but still don't have cash, think back to the reasons set out in chapter 12:

1. You haven't been paid yet (your money is tied up in accounts receivable).

2. You spent it buying assets or repaying debt.

3. You took it as draws.

That's where the cash goes so that's where your reserve will have to come from. Improve your collections, create rules to limit your spending on inventory and other assets, restructure your debt to reduce monthly payments, and take less cash out of the business as draws. Pay attention, be disciplined, and make it happen.

The third required action is to deposit a percentage of each week's sales into the reserve account. You may be able to begin by placing 5 percent of your sales into the reserve account until it is fully funded. However, 5 percent may be too much for your cash-strapped business so you'll have to start with 1 percent or even half of 1 percent of sales (if that's still too much, start with $100). Make weekly deposits based on last week's sales. Do not start your reserve with an overenthusiastic large deposit. If you do, you will almost certainly have to withdraw the funds, which will destroy your reserve—and your resolve—before you even get started.

Most business owners suffer when they delay hard choices. A cash reserve will help you make the hard choices sooner. Where you once had to cut or quit spending because you were out of cash, you will now force yourself to cut or quit spending when cash falls to your target reserve—tougher terms, no inventory expansion, no new assets, no hiring, no draws, and no new overhead expense until the reserve is replenished. Treat the reserve as your new "zero."

As soon as possible, create new, higher reserve targets until you reach a cash reserve equal to three months' cash obligations. The benefits of a cash reserve extend beyond just cash. The process of creating a reserve will make you a more calm, decisive, and effective business owner.

CHAPTER 19

Cashing in on Profit and Confidence: Business Valuation[7]

Who would want it?

—Barbara, a former client and business owner

Your Business Has Value

In at least one respect, investing in real estate and owning a business are alike. Real estate investors benefit from rent in the near term and from appreciation in the value of their holdings over the long term. The opportunity to benefit from both rent *and* appreciation is why real estate investors invest in real estate. Likewise, business owners benefit from profits in the near term and from appreciation of their businesses over the long term. That's the idea, anyway, except it usually doesn't happen.

---

7 In the sale of most small businesses, the buyer does not acquire the seller's actual company. In other words, they do not buy "stock" or ownership units of the existing company. Instead, they acquire the company's assets, including assets that do not appear on the company's balance sheet, such as customer lists, phone numbers, logos, etc. The buyers place the assets into a different business entity through what is known as an asset purchase agreement. The many reasons for this are beyond the scope of this conversation. This discussion of valuation assumes that your company would sell through such an asset purchase transaction.

Virtually every real estate investor is keenly aware of appreciation, but my guess is that only a handful of business owners have any real notion *that* their businesses have value, let alone that the value might appreciate. Businesses do have value and with the right management, the value can appreciate much more and much more quickly than real estate.

In the simplest of terms, the value of a business depends on two variables: Annual profit and buyer confidence. Annual profit is how much money the business earns in a year. Confidence is a measure of how deeply prospective buyers believe the profits will continue or increase after they buy a business. The diligent owner who doubles either profit *or* buyers' confidence doubles the value of the business. The same owner who doubles both profit *and* confidence quadruples the value of the business. Real estate most often appreciates at a steady rate over time. Businesses appreciate as quickly as owners can improve profit and confidence. For that reason, every business owner should understand how businesses are valued and what to do to increase that value.

As you might suspect, given the recurring theme of this book, both proving profits and building confidence begin with proper books. I have had the pleasure of working on several occasions with a business brokerage company called the Hughes Group, which is among the most experienced business brokerage firms in the United States. The company is owned by a dynamic couple, Larry and Beckie Hughes, who have closed on more than 650 business acquisitions over the last 30 years, usually on behalf of the seller. I asked them what single thing helped buyers improve on the companies they bought. I expected to hear answers such as available cash, a dynamic CEO, better marketing, sales training, and synergies with sister companies—that sort of thing. Those are all important contributing factors, but Beckie and Larry answered in unison and immediately, "Experienced business buyers bring in an experienced CFO [Chief Financial Officer]." They went on to explain that CFOs bring an understanding of the numbers that enable managers and owners to make better decisions and more money. Sounds like they agree with the premise of this book, doesn't it?

Has the thought even crossed your mind that your business might have value and someone might want it? If you need persuading, think back to everything you went through to get to where you are today. If for no other reason, buyers want businesses to avoid the pain of going through all that. A buyer acquires your phone number, your reputation, your relationships with vendors and customers, your company culture, your processes, and perhaps your location. You may take all those things for granted but buyers don't. Those things represent a tremendous head start in business that they don't have to recreate. But that's not all.

Sophisticated business buyers understand how to earn extraordinary, *exponential* gains on the businesses they buy. We'll see below why sophisticated buyers *really* want our businesses and how we can benefit from their strategies as owners.

Change Your Thinking; Change Your Future

I first met Barbara and Susan through a course I taught at a community college. Both were in their early sixties and had run their own small businesses for about 20 years. Both businesses were profitable with annual sales of more than $1 million. Although they operated in completely different industries, they had a lot in common, including the fact that they were exhausted.

The business development officer from the local community college recruited them to my course because each told him she was quitting business. Because they were exhausted, they assumed any prospective owner would be too. They planned to auction their equipment and inventory, collect what receivables they could, lock the doors, and walk away.

In the end, the business development officer had done them a great service. Barbara and Susan changed their thinking and transformed their futures. Each worked hard to learn what business buyers want and understand how businesses are valued. They made changes. Rather than settling for "liquidation" value, they made their businesses attractive to buyers as *operating* companies. Barbara sold her business for more than six times the pre-auction estimated proceeds. Susan decided to keep hers.

We should not be surprised that Barbara was able to sell her company, nor that Susan chose to keep hers, because when we build a company that is *attractive to buyers*, we also build a company that is *attractive to us*. When we do things right, reduce our stress load, and increase our cash flow, we may just decide to keep our businesses.

Building Value: Step One

My conversations with hundreds of small business owners tell me most do not believe their businesses have value. Like Susan and Barbara, they are tired and stressed. They either no longer see future opportunities in the companies they've built or they have lost the desire to pursue them. They understand there is value in their inventory, real estate, and other assets, but as for the value of the business itself? They just don't see it.

The first step in business valuation is to believe your business has value. Value begins as a state of mind. Believing enables us to see and pursue higher objectives rather than simply to endure the day-to-day grind of chasing sales, profit, and cash. Believing provides the incentive to learn how businesses are valued, how they are sold, and what we can do to increase their value. Belief is essential but it's not all you need.

Building Value: Step Two

The second step is to understand what buyers want and how they think so we can make our businesses as attractive as possible. Both my experience and my discussions with seasoned business brokers point to five criteria business buyers look for in acquisition targets:

1. Higher-than-normal profit margins for the industry

2. Historic growth and good prospects for continued growth

3. Sales spread over a diverse customer base (not just one or two customers)

4. Stable management (other than us) that will remain with the company after their purchase

5. A system-run company with established processes whose future success does not depend entirely on a precarious few key personnel

We can simplify our discussion by distilling those five criteria into two main conditions: buyers want an appropriate return on their investment and they do not want to acquire a bunch of headaches.

In order to determine the potential return on an investment, buyers will ask sellers to provide current and historic profits and to identify trends. You can't do either without good books. Without good books, the value of your business will plummet and you may lose the sale, as happened to an acquaintance of mine.

I met Dave several years ago through a friend. For the past 12 years, he owned and operated a manufacturing company that made custom windows and doors. The company owned several innovative, proprietary designs and had an excellent reputation for quality and service. Dave told me about his first experience with a prospective buyer, who cited products and reputation as among the reasons he was interested in buying the company.

The man did his research before he called and a tour of the facility convinced him the company's products and reputation were legitimate and exceptional. At the end of the tour, he moved the process along by signing a confidentiality agreement (he brought it with him) and asking to see financial reports.

That was a problem because Dave did not have proper books. His financial recordkeeping consisted of one giant spreadsheet that recorded 12 years' worth of deposits and withdrawals from his bank. His records were of the cash-basis, single-entry sort of books we discussed in chapter 4. Dave described what happened after he opened the spreadsheet and offered the buyer a seat in front of his computer.

After scrolling through the spreadsheet for a few moments, the man got to the point, "How much money did you make last year?"

Dave put the cursor on a cell that showed the difference between deposits and withdrawals for the prior year. "There you go," he said. It was a positive, six-figure number.

"Okay," the man said, "but how much money did you make last year?"

Dave was flummoxed. "That's what we made."

"Maybe, maybe not," the man answered. "That is a pretty good number for a company with 15 employees, but how do I know it's not due to selling inventory this year that you paid for last year?"

"Because it's not," answered Dave.

"But how do I know that? How do *you* know that?" the man asked. "How much inventory did you have on hand last year, and what's your inventory now?"

"About the same," Dave said. At this point, Dave told me he began to get defensive. Defensive is not a good look for a seller answering questions about his business.

"Did you owe your suppliers any money at year-end last year, or have any customer down payment deposits in your bank, or any accounts receivable?"

"Yes, yes, and yes. I'm sure we did," Dave answered. "We always do." Dave couldn't answer how much for any of them.

The man asked a few more questions and left, telling Dave, "I'll get back to you." He called Dave a few weeks later and offered to buy the rights to his proprietary designs. He offered nothing for the business operations. Dave was unwilling to part with critical intellectual property for the price offered, and the negotiations went no further. He was wrecked before he really started because he didn't have proper books and good financial information.

It turns out there are thousands of buyers looking for businesses and competing with each other to buy them. Prospective buyers range from our cross-town competitors to retired businessmen looking for something to do, from our employees to regional firms in our market space to sophisticated equity buyers representing insurance companies, endowment funds, wealthy individuals and families, and so on. The man who bought the last company I sold reportedly had $8 billion in liquid assets. Why in the world would well-funded entities or a man with $8 billion want to buy companies? Because businesses *with the right attributes* are worth more than money in the bank.

To show you what I mean when I say a business is worth more than money, let's say that you take a $100,000 salary from your business. The company earns a profit of $100,000 after your salary and other expenses and you either take or *could take* all of it as draws. In addition to your salary and draws, the business funds another $100,000 in annual benefits, such as your life and health insurance, your retirement fund, your Cadillac Escalade, your daughter's "salary" that pays her college tuition, football tickets, and travel to your annual board meeting in Hawaii. That's $300,000 per year in total owner benefits derived from your company. You would need $15 million[8] in the bank at today's 2 percent interest rates to earn a return of $300,000 per year. (You could probably earn more than 2 percent by investing your sale proceeds in the stock market, but then you'd be back to owning a business.)

Do you have $15 million invested in your business? Probably not, yet the business provides a return as if you did. (Add or subtract zeros to fit your situation, but the logic is the same.) It's clear businesses are worth more than money in the bank, and that's one reason people with money want to buy them.

To understand the second reason, think of a business investment as if it were a real estate investment. Real estate earns rent. Real estate investors value rent because it pays the bills and debt service, but the perhaps bigger incentive for real estate investors is appreciation of their real estate assets over time. They earn rent over the short term and appreciation over the long term. Business investors value profit because, as we've seen, profit is more valuable than money. For sophisticated business owners, however, the bigger incentive is appreciation of the business. Appreciation is less predictable for a business than for real estate, but in the right hands, businesses can appreciate

---

8 $300,000 of interest / 2% annual interest rate = $15 million deposit required.

much more and much more quickly. Real estate assets typically double in value in 10 to 20 years. Skilled business owners can more than double the value of the business in one to three years. We'll see how it works below when we discuss the *real reason buyers want our businesses*.

How much is your business worth? Based on the previous logic, a business that returns $300,000 per year to the owner should be worth $15 million. Buyers ought to be willing to pay $15 million for the business and collect their annual $300,000 from the business instead of the bank. I suppose that's possible but it's also unlikely. People who invest their money in a bank deposit accept a 2 percent return, first because a deposit is a passive investment (they don't have to do any work) and second because they are supremely *confident that the bank will pay them.*

It's different with a business. Business ownership is seldom passive and is also riskier than a bank deposit. The work and the risk mean buyers will demand higher returns from a business investment in order to justify the effort and risk. So how do buyers and sellers adjust value to compensate for the effort and risk?

The details of a particular business valuation can be complicated, but the fundamentals are not. Most businesses are valued as annual profit times a very important number called the "multiple," which we'll discuss below.

$$\text{\$ Profit x Multiple} = \text{\$ Value (Sale Price)}$$

Profit and the multiple are equally important in valuation because each is a factor in a simple multiplication formula. Doubling or tripling either one will double or triple the value of the business. If an owner can double or triple *both*, that would be impressive. We'll see how impressive at the end of this section.

In order to increase the value of our companies, we have to either increase profit or the multiple, or both.

Profit, Defined

Profit is the first factor in valuation and the first source of returns on the buyer's investment. As sellers, we are responsible for profits by the way we operate or more precisely, the way we *have operated* our companies up to the point of sale. Profits and profit trends at the time of sale are what they are and if they are not what we want, then we are not ready to sell our companies. Buyers do not often pay multiples for sales that haven't happened, despite our earnest assurances that they will. Having said that, historically rising sales trends coupled with a rational case for them to continue rising, are very attractive to buyers.

Buyers don't determine past profits but as we saw with Dave's buyer, they will scrutinize them. They will be very interested in profits over the last three years and particularly the last 12 months. They must trust the numbers sellers provide. From the very first introductions through closing, buyers constantly look for assurances that the information and reported profits are real. The first evidence of that is proper books that reconcile with tax returns going back for *at least* three years. Without that evidence, our credibility and the buyer's confidence are weakened and we are at a severe, often terminal, disadvantage in price negotiations.

We have spent the entirety of this book talking about how to use financial reports to improve profits so we won't go through all that again. However, it's important to appreciate that value is calculated as multiple *times* profit, which significantly magnifies the importance of the day-to-day operating decisions that affect profit. A former client's story shows how seemingly insignificant operating decisions can have a disproportionate effect on valuation.

Stephen spent eight years building a software service company with the intent of selling it one day. That day had arrived. After months of negotiations with a sophisticated buyer, Stephen began to change his focus from profit to the value of the company itself.

When a buyer first approached him about selling, Stephen began the negotiations by tossing out what he thought was a high price. There was no particular logic behind it, but if the buyer accepted it, he would be happy, and if they didn't, at least it was a place to start.

The buyers listened politely to his offer, signed a letter indicating their interest and assuring confidentiality, and then began a deliberate process of assessing the value of his company. By the end of their evaluations and after considerable back-and-forth negotiations with Stephen, the parties agreed to a price equal to seven times last year's profits. The price was less than his initial offer but it was a very nice multiple for a small company. It reflected the strength of Stephen's historic marketing, operations, and bookkeeping.

With a defined offer and a letter of intent in hand, Stephen and I began answering due diligence questions. Due diligence is a process of careful investigation by buyers. In very general terms, due diligence requires sellers to answer detailed questions and either to prove by documentation or to attest in writing that their answers are truthful. It's a lengthy, tedious, and exhausting process. (If you're not exhausted by due diligence, it's likely your buyers aren't serious about buying your company.) We had been holed up in Stephen's conference room for hours answering questions and compiling documents when we heard a polite knock at the conference room door.

"Yes?" Stephen said, looking up from his papers.

The door cracked open about a foot, and a young man in his mid-twenties poked his head through the crack.

"Sorry to bother you," he said, "but I left my papers on the projector table. Do you mind if I grab them real quick?"

"Come in," Stephen said sharply. His eyes followed the young man as he crossed the room to get his things and made his way back out the door, closing it softly behind him. It was clear to all three of us that Stephen had been glaring at him.

"That seemed kind of harsh," I said. "Don't worry about the interruption. We'll get through all of this stuff."

"I'm not worried about the interruption," he responded.

"Well, then, what was that all about?' I asked.

"It just dawned on me that he cost me $210,000," Stephen answered.

He was right.

How did an employee who earned a $30,000 salary cost the owner of the business $210,000? From the young man's first week 11 months earlier, Stephen recognized he didn't have the skill or disposition to do his job. He should have let him go, but he hated to fire people, especially the son of a friend. The idea made him so uncomfortable that he decided to absorb the $30,000 salary rather than act. Only it wasn't $30,000. The unnecessary salary reduced profits by $30,000 which, at a seven multiple, reduced the value of his company by $210,000.

Stephen and I had discussed the Profit x Multiple = Value formula many times, but it wasn't until that day in the conference room that he fully realized the cost of his failure to act. The lesson here is to consider the impact of every expense on value, not just profit, and to act accordingly.

Two final points before we move on. First, buyers and sellers, through a process we'll see next, typically "adjust" profits for valuation purposes. These adjustments often work in favor of the seller.

Second, a word of caution about tax avoidance (evasion?). Many of us run our businesses as if our sole purpose in life were to avoid taxes. None of us wants to overpay taxes, and questionable expenses and off-the-books cash sales reduce profit and save taxes in the near term; however, they also reduce valuation by reduced profit *times* the multiple. The value lost to tax avoidance can far exceed the benefit of tax savings.

The True Profit Potential of a Business: Adjusting Profit for Valuation

The value of a business is what a willing seller and buyer agree it to be. There are no laws or absolute rules. However, there are conventional practices, and informed buyers and sellers generally understand and follow them.

The price buyers pay for a business is their investment. Its future profit is a significant source of return on investment. Because buyers are keenly interested in the rate of return on their investment, they will adjust their valuations to match their expectations. For that reason, they spend a great deal of time trying to understand the *true profit potential* of a business they're interested in buying.

When most of us think of profit, we think of the difference between sales and expenses that appears as the bottom line of an income statement. That's the conventional definition, but profit is calculated differently for business valuation.

Why? Because conventional profit may not be a good measure of the true earning capacity of a business. In order to get a clear picture, buyers adjust conventional profit to estimate the *profit potential of the business independent of the current owner, tax rules, and special circumstances.*

You may be thinking, "Yada, yada, yada. Why should we care about such abstract concepts?"

Because buyers care. We may get top dollar for our businesses just by asking, but the chances are we won't. Understanding how buyers think gives us the best shot at the best price.

EBITDA

We won't get far talking valuation before hearing the word EBITDA, an acronym that stands for Earnings Before Interest, Taxes, Depreciation, and Amortization.

The word *earnings* in EBITDA is another name for profit, so EBITDA is what conventional profit would have been had a business not subtracted interest, taxes, depreciation, and amortization expenses on its income statement.

Experienced business buyers estimate true profit potential by performing the following actions:

1. Calculating EBITDA profit for the business

2. Increasing EBITDA by adding back certain expenses

3. Decreasing EBITDA by deducting certain revenue or savings

To calculate EBITDA, we begin with the profit shown on our income statement and "add back" interest, tax, depreciation, and amortization expenses. EBITDA will likely be higher than conventional profit, sometimes a lot higher. EBITDA is a useful number because interest, taxes, depreciation, and amortization expenses—and therefore, profit—can vary widely for the same business, depending on who owns it.

Interest and Taxes Depend on the Owner

The amounts of interest and tax expense incurred by a business directly affect profit but depend heavily on the decisions of a particular owner.

Interest

A cash-poor owner may borrow heavily and incur significant interest expense to fund the business. A cash-rich owner may not borrow any money or incur *any* interest expense to fund the same business. Cash-poor or cash-rich, interest or no interest, or any combinations of those factors depend on the owner, not the business.

Taxes

The "T" for taxes in EBITDA refers to state and federal income taxes, not sales tax, property taxes, or other tax expense a business might incur. We add back income taxes if they have been deducted as expenses because, like interest, the amount of taxes paid depends heavily on current tax law, the owner's tax position, and the owner's choice of legal structure of the business—none of which can be blamed on the business itself. We do not add back sales taxes, property taxes, and other possible taxes to EBITDA because they are the same, regardless of who owns the business.

We should be aware that, depending on the legal structure of the business, there may not be any income tax expenses listed on our income statements, even though we paid a lot of income taxes.

Noncash expenses

We add back depreciation and amortization expenses not only because they depend on owner's choices but also because they are "noncash" expenses.

Depreciation

Depreciation is an expense, a "write-off," that is allowed by the tax authorities to acknowledge that tangible assets such as buildings, trucks, and equipment wear out or become obsolete. Businesses don't actually pay depreciation as they would a utility bill, but they are allowed to deduct depreciation expense as if they did.

The deducted amount of depreciation expense depends on tax rules and owners' choices that seldom matches reality. Assets are usually written off either much faster or much more slowly than they really wear out or become obsolete. Therefore, depreciation is simply an accounting entry, a noncash expense, that does not reflect the true cost of wear or obsolescence and distorts the true earning capacity of a business.

Amortization

Amortization is depreciation for intangible assets. Intangible assets are things a business owns that we can't touch, including patent rights, goodwill, or franchise rights. Our businesses may not have intangible assets but many do. Amortization, like depreciation, is an accounting entry and a noncash expense.

Other Add-Backs

Interest, taxes, depreciation, and amortization add-backs are well understood so we shouldn't expect any resistance making the adjustments. However, special circumstances unique to a business may result in other add-back possibilities. The possibilities include unusual or one-time expenses that are not likely to repeat or expenses charged to the business that are really benefits to the owner. These adjustments are subject to negotiations, which might go something like this:

Seller: "I paid myself a $100,000 annual salary. I'm leaving, so you won't have that expense. Let's *add back* my salary to profit!"

Buyer: "Not so fast. I have to pay someone to replace you, so no, no add-back."

Seller: "But you can easily replace me with someone for $75,000."

Buyer: "So you say…"

or

Seller: "We need to adjust last year's travel expense. We made three 'business' trips to Europe"—wink, wink—"and held our annual board meeting in Hawaii. Staying here would have reduced travel expenses by $45,000, which would increase last year's profit by the same amount. There are also the expenses for the company Escalade I drive, the life insurance the business pays for me, and the…"

Do you get the idea? Sellers make the case to add back expenses to increase profit; buyers resist. Every negotiation is different, so we can't anticipate specifically how each one will go. It is a good idea to plan for a sale and eliminate optional expenses in advance of negotiations.

You may be thinking, "Woo-hoo! Good for us. We like adjustments!" But hold on. There's a flip side. Up to this point, we've been doing a lot of adding back, which has worked in our favor. But we can't expect a buyer to just sit there and take it. Buyers will look for certain types of "deductions" to subtract from profit and lower the valuation. These deductions, like add-backs, are subject to negotiations, which might go like this:

Buyer: "You owned your building and didn't pay rent. I'm going to adjust profit down to reflect rent expense."

Seller: "But I'm selling the building to you. You won't have rent."

Buyer: "True, but I'll have interest on the mortgage."

Seller: "It's not my fault you have to borrow to buy the building…"

or

Buyer: "A big chunk of last year's profit came from that one sale to your brother-in-law. That's not likely to happen again, so I'm going to reduce profit by—"

Seller: "True, but we have three big sales in the pipeline, all teed up and ready to go."

Buyers will continue to make their case by arguing, for example, that our stated profit is too high because we neglected maintenance or didn't replace obsolete equipment or reduced our marketing budget to inflate profits, and so on.

Now you might be thinking, "Hold on a minute. I've looked at my profit and likely adjustments, and even if I win all the negotiations, my business is worth a lot more than two or three times adjusted annual profit. Heck, my building alone is worth way more than that, not to mention my cash, inventory, and accounts receivable." Excellent point. We'd better define what we're valuing when we value "the business."

Think of a business as a truck. A truck earns profit by hauling freight, just as a business does by doing whatever it does. We all recognize that the value of the truck doesn't include the parking lot, the cargo on board, or money due for freight hauled in the past. The same is true of a business. The value of a business as determined by the $ Profit x Multiple = $ Value formula doesn't include real estate, cash, inventory, or accounts receivable.

If owners also sell their real estate, accounts receivable, and inventory, those values would be added to the value of the business to determine the total price of the transaction.

"Woo-hoo! Good for us again! Add-backs and now add-ons?" Yes, but let's use the truck analogy to look at one more thing—debt. When you sell your truck, the buyer expects to receive a free and clear title, unencumbered by your debt. The same is true of a business. If we still have business-related debt, that's on us. It won't affect the price a buyer pays, but it will affect our net proceeds because sellers keep and pay off their debt.

Remember, the value of a business is what a willing buyer and seller agree it to be. Although buyers and sellers do not have to follow the conventions described above, they nonetheless provide insight into how *experienced* business buyers think. Understanding experienced buyers gives us the best shot at getting the best price for our businesses. To prepare for and anticipate a negotiated profit, you must:

1. Calculate EBITDA profit

2. Increase EBITDA by anticipated add-backs

3. Protect EBITDA by limiting negotiated deductions

4. Add cash, accounts receivable, inventory, and real estate to the value of the business (and to the price if the buyer is acquiring them too)

5. Anticipate that we, not the buyer, will have to pay debt, so subtract the debt from the expected proceeds of the sale (not the price) of the business

Multiple Defined

So that's profit, but what is the multiple all about? The multiple is a measure of a buyer's confidence. It's a valuation method for adjusting price up or down. A business with an annual profit of $100,000 valued at a multiple of two would be worth $200,000. Double the multiple to four and we double the value to $400,000. It's obvious that the multiple is a pretty important number, but how do we determine it? The short answer is "through negotiations." A more precise answer is "risk assessment."

Risk is a big deal in any investment negotiation, and business valuation is no exception. The multiple is the business valuation equivalent of an interest rate. I don't know why business valuations are expressed in multiples rather than interest, but they are. When you buy a Certificate of Deposit at a bank, you expect a return on your investment in the form of *guaranteed* interest payments. Business buyers expect a return, too, and their returns come from *anticipated* profits. The difference between "guaranteed" and "anticipated" future profits is risk, and it is a very big deal in valuation.

The higher the risk, the higher the return buyers will demand as compensation. That makes sense. If your brother-in-law wants you to invest in his harebrained start-up company, you would demand a much higher return from him than from the bank; otherwise, you'd just buy that nice, safe CD. A risky investment must pay more than a safe investment in order to attract buyers. How much more is reflected in the multiple. To see how it works, look at the example below.

If your bank offers a 10 percent annual interest rate (not likely these days, but the math is easier) and you bought a CD for $1,000, you would receive a $100 annual payment. That's how people normally think about investments: A certain investment times a rate of return gives the amount of return. Instead of telling you about the interest rate, a business buyer might say that she bought the CD for a 10 multiple ($100 return x 10 = $1,000 price of the CD).

Business buyers make an estimate of the expected return (future profits) and then adjust the valuation (their investment) until the rate of return is appropriate to the risk. To illustrate what I mean, let's look again at the CD example. Instead of offering an interest rate, suppose your bank offered an investment promising to pay you $100 each year. How much would you pay for that? If you're happy with 10 percent, you'd pay $1,000, or *10 times the annual payment.* You're happy with that 10 multiple because banks are safe. But what about your brother-in-law?

Suppose your crazy brother-in-law offers to sell you a share in his start-up company for $1,000. He earnestly assures you that you will earn $100 per year (a 10 percent annual return on your investment) in future profits, but you're not so sure. If you buy into his company, it's an investment like the CD, only this time your return must come from future profits. Given what you know about your brother-in-law, you're not inclined to accept a 10 percent return on your $1,000. So how much would you pay? Family issues aside, certainly not a 10 multiple. In vivid contrast to the bank, his start-up is anything but safe. You judge his venture to be so risky that you offer him $100 for an investment that will (maybe) pay you $100 per year. That's a one multiple, which is equivalent to a 100 percent return each year on your $100 investment. Such is your perception of the risk associated with your brother-in-law.

That's how it's done in business valuation. Buyers estimate the amount and likelihood of future profits and then adjust their offer price until the rate of return is appropriate to their estimate of risk. Then I suppose because it makes for easy price calculations, they express the rate of return as an equivalent multiple. The graph below shows various interest rates and their equivalent multiples. You can see the dramatic effect of risk. The higher the perceived risk, the higher the rate of return buyers demand and the lower the multiple they will offer.

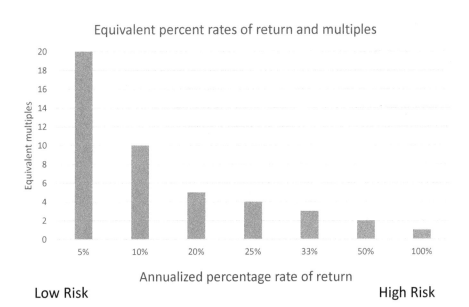

Equivalent percent rates of return and multiples

Buyers demand a higher percentage return on their investment in a risky business as compared to a less risky business. The graph shows clearly: As risk goes up, multiples go down, and as risk goes down, multiples go up. Dramatically. To increase the value of your business, you must inspire confidence in prospective buyers to reduce their perceived risk. Confidence *always* begins with proper books.

The Real Reason Buyers Want Our Businesses

Buyers want businesses because the right businesses are worth more than money. But that's not all. Sophisticated business buyers understand that business values based on profit times a multiple offer the opportunity for extraordinary, exponential returns on their investments that far exceed those from profits alone.

To understand how they think, assume a sophisticated buyer purchases a business making $100,000 per year at a two multiple. The arithmetic looks like this:

Beginning value:

$100,000 profit x 2 multiple = $200,000 valuation

They put their considerable skills to work doing the things the sellers knew they should have done but didn't. They make the changes in the first year of ownership. Their efforts double profit and, therefore, the value of the business. That is a 100 percent return on the value of their investment in one year. And that's in addition to the profit itself!

$200,000 x 2 multiple = $400,000 valuation

That's nice, but that's not all—not by a long shot. Let's say the buyer puts in systems and controls, brings in an experienced president, a chief financial officer, a professional marketing firm, improves margins and inventory turns, and provides some needed working capital. The actions make the company more stable and attractive, which doubles the multiple along with the profits. The two together increase the value of the business by four times, a 400 percent return on the original investment in one year—and again, that's in addition to profit!

Double profit and double multiple value:

$200,000 profit x 4 multiple = $800,000 valuation

A buyer who triples profit *and* triples the multiple would increase the value of the business by *nine times*! This is the compound effect of increasing both profit and the multiple.

If that all sounds too good to be true, it's not. Exponential growth is the real reason private equity firms, hedge funds, and investment bankers want our businesses. When they buy companies, they immediately and deliberately set out to increase the value of the business by increasing both profit and the multiple. It's what they do. It's why they exist.

We Don't Have to Be Investment Bankers

We can do it too! We don't have to be investment bankers to benefit from exponential growth in equity, but we do have to recognize the opportunity and act to increase both profit and multiple.

We have to think like sophisticated business buyers. That means we must begin well in advance, usually at least three years in advance, to protect and grow our profits. We must also do what's necessary to assure future buyers that they are buying a return on their investment and not just a job.

Good books are essential to reporting our profits, our growth, our customer concentration, and our trends. Proper books are the first evidence of a system-run business and are fundamental to building confidence in buyers. We cannot expect to do well in negotiations without them.

One Last Thing to Consider

Once we've built a business to sell, it's time to ask ourselves if we really want to do that. As we saw with Barbara and Susan, there are two main reasons owners want out: To cash in on the value of the business or to shed the burdens of ownership. Do those reasons sound familiar? It turns out that buyers and sellers are *looking for the same things*—a good return on investment and freedom from the daily grind. When we build a business that's attractive to buyers, we also build a business that's attractive to us. So should we keep it or sell it?

Susan and Barbara answered that question differently. Barbara sold her business. Susan kept hers. Susan took deliberate steps to make the business more attractive to buyers and wound up making it attractive to herself. She installed good books and systems, which contributed to a 25 percent increase in net profits. She hired a general manager to run day-to-day operations and devoted 100 percent of her time to dealing with large customers, which is her passion. After building a company to sell, she realized she had eliminated her reasons for selling.

When considering whether or not to sell, it's important to remember that a business is worth more than money in the bank. We are unlikely to earn as much from sales proceeds as we would if we kept the business. If that's true and we've built a business run by good management (other than ourselves) and delegated our operational headaches, why not keep it?

The lesson here is that, regardless of what we think we may do in the future, we should build a business that will sell, and the first step is to have proper books.

CHAPTER 20

Embezzlement

A person may cause evil to others not only by his actions but also by his inaction.

—John Stuart Mill, *On Liberty*

I said earlier that if you make money but don't have any, there are three possible reasons: You haven't been paid yet, you already spent it paying down debt or buying assets, or you took it. Well, unfortunately, there is a fourth possibility: Somebody else took it. The Association of Certified Fraud Examiners (ACFE) reported that businesses in 2018 lost 5 percent of *sales* to occupational fraud,[9] the majority of which was embezzlement. Small businesses earn an average of 7 percent of sales net profit, which means fraud is either wiping them out or reducing their returns by more than half.

If you don't think it can happen to you, there's a good chance that it already has. It happened to me.

Protecting Yourselves *and Them*

"It's me, Martin. It's all me."

"How far back should I go?"

"January."

---

9 "Report to The Nations 2018 Global Study on Occupational Fraud and Abuse," The Association of Certified Fraud Examiners, https://s3-us-west-2.amazonaws.com/acfepublic/2018-report-to-the-nations.pdf.

I went back to January but I didn't stop there. By the time I'd been through five years of bank statements, I found more than $340,000 missing, stolen by the *most trusted* member of our management team—our in-house bookkeeper. (The ACFE reports that the median theft from companies with fewer than 100 employees is $200,000. I generally like to rank above average but not this time!) In the end, her father paid back the money, but she got jail time and ruined not only her life but the lives of those most dear to her as well.

Our bookkeeper stole from us through a very simple process: She paid her credit cards online using our bank accounts. I didn't catch on because we had a lot of credit cards and hers was issued from the same bank as the company's. The only thing that distinguished her card from ours was the account number, which did not stand out on our bank statements. I didn't notice her account number among ours until she took a very large sum in one month.

Looking back, there were many signs I should have noticed but didn't because I trusted her and couldn't imagine her ever stealing from the company. *It never even occurred to me to check.* Although she made the decision to do it, *I allowed* the environment that made her theft possible. I could have prevented the theft but I didn't, and for that reason, as John Stuart Mill said above, I am at least partly responsible not only for her ruined life but also for those of her family.[10] It is our responsibility as business owners to prevent embezzlement. Not only for the sake of our companies (I think back to the many times we could have used that $340,000!) but also for the sake of the individuals impacted.

Don't think it won't happen to you. Ask around, and you will find that embezzlement in business is as common as dirt. So common that the detective scoffed at my meager $340,000 claim. He told me his white-collar crime division had enough multimillion-dollar claims lined up to consume the department's entire resources into the foreseeable future. He said the only way they would pursue my case was if I would lay out the facts and evidence in foolproof detail, which I did. But all too often, embezzlement tracks have

---

10 She was sentenced to jail for the theft, among other penalties and consequences.

been well covered, making prosecution unlikely and reimbursement even less likely. This is why preventing embezzlement with the right attitude, knowledge, and procedures can save your business and employees tremendous loss.

Attitude: Trust but Verify

We must maintain the attitude that embezzlement is not only possible but also likely because it is. Everyone in our organizations should know we are constantly watching and have procedures in place to prevent theft. It's not personal. It's business.

The message is zero tolerance. Adopt the attitude that theft is theft. It doesn't matter if it involves many thousands of dollars or a meal charged on the company credit card. Theft is theft, and we will not tolerate it.

Knowledge: Motives and Methods

Most embezzlers don't intend to become thieves[11] and almost always start out small. My bookkeeper, for example, had a family emergency and took a few hundred dollars, intending to return it. She paid back a little but over time "forgot" to pay back the balance. Nobody noticed, and something else came up. She took a little more, still intending to pay it back. Again, nobody noticed. Over time, she dropped all pretense of "borrowing," and family emergencies become clothes, vacations, and cars.

As for methods,[12] those of us who don't think like thieves are often surprised at how embezzlers do it. We are even more surprised at how easy it is. If you are familiar at all with basic accounting controls, the following methods will seem pretty simple, but they worked. Some real-life examples include:

---

11 Of course, the thief might just be a greedy, low-life SOB.
12 For an in-depth look at preventing fraud, read the book, *The Complete Guide to Spotting Accounting Fraud & Cover-Ups,* by Martha Maeda.

- *Deposit and delete.* This is the scheme we saw when we met my neighbor in chapter 17. Joe's bookkeeper set up a company with a name similar to his company's. When customers paid their accounts, she deposited the checks to the dummy company and deleted the original sales transaction from QuickBooks. Poof! Transaction and money were gone.

- *Sweetheart check.* A bookkeeper responsible for payroll paid her boyfriend $600 per month as contract labor for work he didn't do. He never even showed up to work.

- *Supplier charges.* This is so common, it's almost universal. The employee buys gas or supplies or material for personal use on the company account.

- *Phony invoices.* An employee working with someone at a supplier business accepts and pays phony invoices for materials or services never received.

- *Dummy companies.* A manager with complete signing authority set up maintenance and landscaping companies to care for properties she managed. The companies charged over $300,000 for work not done.

- *Disappearing cash.* It's harder to steal cash these days because so many payments are made with cards and transfers, but cash regularly disappears from restaurants, bars, and convenience stores. The most common method is to pocket cash for transactions that are never rung up.

- *Prior-year entries.* I would have noticed my bookkeeper's thefts had she entered them as expenses in the current month. She didn't. She entered the "expenses" in prior years and then transferred them back at year-end. I didn't notice the charges after they had been transferred back because the amounts were not noticeable mixed in among large annual totals.

Procedures: Prevention Over Panic

Most of those problems could have been prevented by simply paying attention. However, we seldom have time to monitor every credit card transaction, check, bill, and receivable. We can't haphazardly review transactions, especially *if we don't have proper books.* We can and must find the time to install antitheft processes and to devote several hours each month to reviewing a few critical reports. Below are some examples of basic processes used to prevent or catch embezzlement.

- *Reconcile bank accounts.* At the absolute bare minimum, we have to reconcile our bank accounts every month. Without reconciled bank statements, we have almost no chance of spotting theft. To be effective, we have to reconcile while charges and deposits are fresh in our minds.

- If we are unable or unwilling to reconcile our own bank accounts, we have to find someone to do it for us, but that someone should *not* be the same person who pays the bills. It's best to get an outside accountant to reconcile our accounts.

- *Reconcile credit card statements.* Credit cards are just like bank statements and should be reconciled for the same reasons. Again, the cards should not be reconciled by the same person who makes charges or who pays the credit card bills.

- *Keep good books.* This is the most important defense of all. "Good books" means up-to-date, double-entry, accrual-basis books, such as the system offered by QuickBooks. Keeping good books includes reviewing the information they provide.

- *Have an outside accountant review and close books each month.* Very few small businesses review and close their books every month but doing so provides the best systematic process for reviewing recent transactions. Closing books makes it difficult for embezzlers to backdate transactions, as my bookkeeper did, or to delete past transactions to cover theft.

- *Get receipts.* Every transaction in business begins with a source document. At a minimum, we need receipts for all expenses that show *what* was purchased, not just *where* it was purchased.

- *Separation of duties.* The person who does our invoicing should not receive payments on account. The person who enters bills should not pay bills. The person who receives cash should not deposit cash in the bank.

- *Signature authority.* We should all guard our signature authority closely. Signature authority applies to paper checks, bank transfer authority, and whatever other authority permits people to transfer money from or among our bank accounts.

- *Bill review.* Paying bills should be a formal process. Good books enable us to print accounts payable, which we should review and use to choose which bills to pay at any given time.

- *Accounts receivable review.* Good books enable us to print accounts receivable listings, which we should review at least monthly.

For harried small business owners, that sounds like a lot, but it really isn't. Most of us can do it by establishing a few procedural changes and devoting a few hours a month to reviews. It's simple when it becomes routine. Work with your accountant to develop the right procedures for your business.

Our obligation to prevent theft extends beyond ourselves and our companies to include others. People need to know we are always looking. We want to communicate that it's the way we do things around here, and we're not changing.

CHAPTER 21

KPIs: Key Performance Indicators

To solve a problem, you must first measure it.

—Ola Rosling, Swedish statistician, coauthor of
Factfulness and cofounder of Gapminder.org

KPIs (Key Performance Indicators) are numbers that signal what's important to you and provide benchmarks to measure how well you're progressing toward a goal. KPIs can be simple—sales and profit are both KPIs—or they can be more sophisticated and capture your company values and philosophy, as we'll see below.

Management Requires Measurement

Edward Deming, one of the great thinkers in business management, is quoted saying, "If you do not measure it, you cannot manage it." The corollary to that statement is: if you don't manage it, everything that happens to you—good or bad—is an accident.

KPIs provide measurements expressed in numbers, often in the form of ratios. Numbers tell us what we *need* to know, whether we *want* to know or not.

For example, compare the following statements: "Sales per employee are up from \$119,500 per year to \$141,200 per year." "I feel pretty good about employee productivity this year." The first is useful. Just by reading the numbers, everyone will know you are measuring them and what is important to you. That information alone will have a positive effect. But even more, you can use the information to identify specific activities to improve, reward employees, evaluate a sales initiative, direct future expenditures, build shareholder confidence, and more. The second statement is not useful at all. Heck, you might feel good because it's a pretty day—but then, what is a "pretty day?"

Everything in business can be measured objectively in numbers. Some things are easy to measure because your accounting already tracks sales, profit, accounts receivable, accounts payable, gross margins, net worth, cash flow, and the like. Some things are harder to measure because accounting doesn't track them directly, but you have information such as average transaction in dollars, sales per employee, units produced per month, leads-to-sales conversions, lifetime value of a customer, inventory turns, and days outstanding for accounts receivable. Other things are even more difficult to measure because you have to define, gather, and quantify the information. These include such things as quality, reputation, customer satisfaction, employee attitude, leadership, and happiness.

What Gets Measured Gets Better

Selecting and tracking KPIs requires thought and effort, but I will say again that what gets measured gets better. I have personally observed that with many of my clients, but you don't have to take my word for it. Jim Collins, author of *Good to Great* says, "Every Good-to-Great company built a fabulous economic engine…because they attained profound insights into their economics." The insights were provided by what Collins calls "denominators"—in other words, ratios used as KPIs.

KPIs are like stats in sports. It wouldn't do for a basketball coach to simply yell at his defeated team, "Do better!" But if the same coach sees a stat showing his team is weak in free throw percentages, he can develop a drill to help them improve and both he and they can track their progress.

To see how it works in business, think back to Eli's, the pool service we met in chapter 14. Eli's had a lot of sales but slim profits. What were they to do?

Recall that we chose to track a weekly KPI of billed man-hours divided by paid man-hours that we named "labor productivity rate." The initial KPI was 32 percent, which meant that 68 percent of technician payroll hours were not billed to customers. The KPI quantified a problem, provided a benchmark to improve upon, and an objective means to reward employees for improvement. By working with technicians, the owners found that poor scheduling, inefficient routing, forgotten parts, "comped" hours, late starts, "go-backs," schedule-wrecking "add-on" work, and long lunches were factors—all specific activities that could be tracked and improved upon.

We were also surprised to discover unbilled hours resulting from a practice common among technicians. When one technician finished his job early, he would travel to help a second technician at another location. Having two technicians on-site sped up the job and reduced the hours billed by the first technician. Although it was great teamwork, there was a problem: The second technician didn't bill for his hours. The result was fewer total hours billed and a lower labor productivity rate. (That's the sort of nonobvious problem you will uncover when you start looking.) Today, the technicians still help each other but they bill for their combined hours.

The company now provides a weekly incentive to technicians when they meet or exceed a labor productivity rate of 50 percent billed hours. You can see how the KPI provided the insight necessary to come up with specific activities that made a difference—and what a difference! This case is a work-in-progress so we don't know exactly how much things will improve. But we do know this: had last year's ratio improved from 32 percent to just 50 percent, net profit would have been 419 percent higher!

We found an immensely relevant and useful KPI at Eli's. To find yours, ask yourself: What is my priority?[13] What do I need to improve on that will have the greatest impact on my business at this time? What is a KPI that will benchmark my current condition and provide insights, suggest actions for improvement, and provide a score for measuring them? Identify your priority, then work with your accountant and team to create a meaningful KPI and to come up with specific actions to improve it.

Your KPI might be a conventional number that captures the purely objective information, such as Eli's labor productivity ratio, or it could be the time it takes to collect an account receivable, the number of times you turn your inventory each month or year, or the cost of acquiring a new customer. Your KPI might be unconventional and unique to you and your business. Your KPI might even signal your values and philosophy.

A well-known outdoor clothing company's philosophy is to use business to inspire and implement solutions to the environmental crisis. They measure their impact on the environment by tracking the percentage of material sourced through sustainable methods, and they even discourage their customers from buying too many of their products! That is their philosophy, and it appeals not to only to their team but to their customers. (Of course, they have to charge more for their products to pay for sustainability and fewer sales to customers, and they're pretty good at that too.)

My all-time favorite KPI is the BMW KPI—as in the car, a smart-driving, all-wheel drive, six-cylinder, fully tricked-out BMW 440. I refer to the BMW KPI as an "abundance" KPI that captures and highlights an important accomplishment. Lance, my oldest client, and I measure it every Friday morning at 11:00 and we have for more than three years.

Lance is a genius in his technical field, so much so that when we talk about his technology, I usually don't understand what he is talking about. Lance was very good at his original business, but for a variety of reasons, he

---

13 In his must-read book, *The ONE Thing: The Surprisingly Simple Truth Behind Extraordinary Results,* author and Keller Williams CEO Gary William points out that the word *priority* means "first." There cannot be more than one first; therefore, you cannot, and should not, have more than one priority at a time at your work.

didn't enjoy it. He decided four years ago to remake his business into one he could enjoy and he did. However, because he was always concerned that things might go wrong, he never rewarded himself for his success. He had not given himself a raise in 10 years and he took very little cash out of the company as draws. He was reluctant to do so because of "what-ifs"—as in, "What if I lose all my customers to an economic downturn?" or "What if my competitors overtake me?" (You know about that sort of thinking, right?)

The BMW KPI number is the cash balance in one of his bank accounts. About two years ago the balance reached a six-figure milestone. I congratulated him and suggested he do something to reward himself. I knew from our many conversations that he wanted a BMW so I suggested he buy one. I could tell his resistance was flagging when, instead of giving me all the reasons he couldn't, he responded, "That's what my wife said."

Four days after our conversation, a photo popped up in a text on my phone: There was Lance standing next to his brand-new BMW 440. Bingo! He did it. He was still concerned that he had made a mistake, that a "what-if" would happen and he would regret the purchase. That's why we began tracking the BMW KPI. I'm happy to report that since he bought the car, the bank balance has *tripled*.

The KPI transformed his thinking. He is still conservative but the BMW KPI prompted an abundance mindset. He believes he can both survive professionally and benefit personally. He has hired more *great* people in the two years since we began tracking the KPI than in the previous 10 years because he has the confidence to pay for great employees. He has invested in serious marketing and has delegated important duties to his new hires (both of which he was very reluctant to do before the KPI)—and all the while, the BMW KPI and his confidence continue to grow.

What is your priority? What one thing, if improved, would have the greatest impact on your business and life? Everybody and every business has one. Give some thought to your priority and how to create a KPI to measure it. It will be worth the effort because "by accident" is not a worthwhile management strategy.

We've reached the point at which you recognize proper books, you understand why they are important, and how they can relieve suffering by helping you make better decisions and more money. The next step is to begin.

CHAPTER 22

How to Begin Keeping Good Books: Starting from Wherever You Are

The secret of getting ahead is getting started.

—Unknown (attributed to Mark Twain)

T HE JOB OF TRANSFORMING BOOKS FROM WHATEVER THEY ARE INTO A useful set of proper books is one of the most consistently frustrating tasks I encounter with new clients. The job often drags on for months or even years—first because clients are distracted by day-to-day operations and second because they have neither the knowledge nor incentive to get the job done. That's why I said in the introduction you should read this book in order to recognize proper books and to understand how they will help you make better decisions and more money. You've read the book, can you recognize proper books? Do you have a burning desire to acquire them for your business? So now what? How do you begin?

Whether you've been keeping inadequate books for years or you are just beginning to keep books, the seven-step process is the same.

Step 1: Hire a qualified accountant. Do *not* try to transform or set up your books yourself. It would not be the best use of your time and you don't have the knowledge or experience to do it well. (If you did, you would already have good books.)

Any good CPA or really good bookkeeper *can* set up useful books for your company but be forewarned: Most *won't*. I have countless examples of accountants who take on the task but never complete it. You will have to interview accountants to find one who is enthusiastic and committed to helping you. Here are some questions to ask prospective accountants:

- What does accounting mean to you?

- What is breakeven, and how can you use it?

- How do you forecast cash requirements for your clients?

- What expenses should be included in cost of goods sold?

- What key ratios do you routinely provide to your clients?

- What routine steps would you take to prevent embezzlement?

- Do you *enjoy* working throughout the year to help business clients make operating decisions?

- Do you have systems and processes to routinely close books for your clients?

Step 2: Establish a completion date for the project. Without a deadline, bookkeeping projects always seem to mush on indefinitely. Set a date, stick to it, and hold everyone involved accountable for getting it done properly and on time.

Step 3: Keep up your end of the bargain. This is *your* project and *your* priority. The number one reason accountants don't complete projects on schedule is that business owners do not give them the information they need.

Step 4: The accountant must reconcile your entire balance sheet using the processes described in chapter 17. Good books *always* begin with a balance sheet that is correct as of a specific date. The bad news is that this will be a tedious and annoying process. The good news is that, once it's done, you will have accurate, current, and useful information that will be much easier to maintain than it was to compile.

Step 5: The accountant must organize your profit and loss statement. The accountant should separate your overhead expenses from cost of goods sold expenses so you can see your margins and know your breakeven. He or she will reclassify miscategorized items and will make bookkeeping entries to best match income with expenses.

Step 6: Your bookkeeper must work with the accountant to write out processes detailing how and when to make routine bookkeeping entries. At a minimum, you should receive written, step-by-step instructions explaining how to perform the following activities in your bookkeeping software:

1. Invoice customers
2. Receive payments from customers
3. Make bank deposits
4. Enter bills
5. Pay bills
6. Enter and pay credit card charges
7. Separate and record interest and principal for loan payments
8. Track inventory
9. Make inventory adjustments
10. Separate overhead expense from cost of goods sold
11. Make adjustments to match sales and expenses
12. Handle customer prepayment deposits
13. Preserve receipts for expenses
14. Make monthly depreciation entries

Those are a lot of processes but once established, they quickly become routine.

Step 7: As we saw in chapter 17, your accountant should set up a process for closing your books each month by reconciling all the accounts on the balance sheet and by checking the profit and loss statement for matching issues and misplaced entries. Closing your books every month ensures that the information you rely on is current and accurate. It keeps you current on the condition of your business and protects against embezzlement. Monthly closing also makes tax and cash planning possible and provides a recent benchmark to refer to when looking for bookkeeping errors, which are inevitable.

If you don't keep books, or if you don't use your books because you know they are inaccurate, you are missing out on the most powerful tool in business management. If you are convinced that proper books can relive your suffering, free up your time, and help you make more money, get started. Today. Without you as a committed, dedicated champion, it will never happen.

We are nearly at the end, but before we finish, I want you to know how much I appreciate small business owners and managers and how *important* you are not only to me but also to the world as *the* source of abundance.

CHAPTER 23

Business: The Temporal Source of Abundance

Toiling—rejoicing—sorrowing
Onward through life he goes:
Each morning he sees some task begin,
Each evening he sees it close.
Something attempted, something done,
He has earned his night's repose.

—Henry W. Longfellow, "The Village Blacksmith"

I LOVE SMALL BUSINESS OWNERS. THEY WAKE UP EVERY MORNING AND shoulder their burdens, often alone, always at personal risk and they do it without any assurance of reward. They put others' interests ahead of their own (they may not intend it that way but that's the way it works), they contribute mightily to the abundance that surrounds us, and they often do it with few resources beyond courage and determination.

The Evidence

I first came to appreciate the importance of small business in 1976 as I stood looking out the window in Denver's Stapleton International Airport. I had just finished reading a book describing an immense fire in 1864. The fire began along a line that crossed the Nebraska-Colorado border and eventually burned an entire prairie between the Platte and Republican Rivers, a vast area covering nearly 30,000 square miles.

The story was fresh in my mind because I lived in Nebraska and traveled that day along Interstate 80, following the path of the historic fire. I arrived early at the airport and spent an hour watching airplanes when it occurred to me that the ground beneath me had probably burned in that fire.

Less than 120 years later, where there had been fire, and buffalo and horses, there were now airplanes—hundreds of them departing, arriving, taxiing, and sitting parked on acres of concrete. The airplanes were tangible evidence of countless discoveries and untold hours spent engineering, testing, and refining the components that make up an airplane. Beyond that, there had been many other discoveries and hours spent developing the principles, procedures, and standards that make flight possible.

I could go on and on about technology, flight schedules, airport food, and the glass in the window I was looking through. All were among the uncountable advances that made it possible for me to fly to San Francisco that day in search of a deal.

As the realizations piled in on me, I began to question where it had all come from. I decided against the notion that people had actually created anything new. After all, there is nothing on earth today that wasn't here in 1864 or ten thousand or even ten million years ago.[14] Without question, all those developments occurred through the conversion of existing resources into more useful forms.

Usefulness doesn't just appear. It is the result of resources finding their way into the hands of people who have the means and talent to convert them into more useful forms. A miner's ore is more useful for having passed

---

14 It is not strictly true that there is nothing on earth that wasn't here ten million years ago. The weight of the earth increases by about forty thousand tons per year from stardust attracted by its gravity. However, I stand by my point.

through the hands of a smelter who converted it into aluminum, which is more useful for having passed through the hands of a processor who rolled it into sheets, which are more useful still for having passed through the hands of an aircraft maker who shaped them into the skin of an airplane.

Those, and all the other useful conversions swirling around us, are the results of transactions between parties, each of which received something it valued more than what it gave up in the exchange. Transaction after transaction and benefit compounding benefit until we reached the point that air travel, cellular telephones, and the internet are routine.

The collective transactions that took us from horses to airplanes comprise commerce, which we call business. The gain from transactions we call profit. Business and mutual profit are uniquely human. To paraphrase Adam Smith,[15] no dolphin has freely exchanged a squid for two mackerel with the intent or effect of profiting both itself and its dolphin buddy. Only people do that, and it has resulted in the staggering gains I saw that day in Denver and in the promise of infinitely more to come.[16]

Neither business nor profit would be possible without government, financial systems, armies, courts, universities, and myriad other institutions that make business possible. But it is through business that transactions originate, and it is from a portion of profits that all the other indispensable institutions draw their sustenance. That places business—along with the bookkeeping that makes business possible—squarely at the source of abundance.

---

15 *An Inquiry into the Nature and Causes of the Wealth of Nations* by Adam Smith (1776).
16 For a fascinating, beautifully researched, and easy-to-read book about the history of modern man and our future prospects, read Matt Ridley's book, *The Rational Optimist: How Prosperity Evolves.* The future is much brighter than you may think.

GLOSSARY

If I'd known the difference between an antidote and an anecdote,
ole Billy Johnson would still be alive today.
—Ron White

Definitions

If you're going to speak the language of business, it helps to know the words. Below are definitions of some financial terms you will encounter in bookkeeping and financial discussions.

Financial terms are often used loosely, and I am never reluctant to ask a speaker or financial professional what he or she means when using terms such as "cash flow," "margins, or "profit." If in doubt, ask. You will benefit from clarity and you will appear more intelligent for having asked.

Accounts — A record of financial expenditures or receipts organized into groups according to the person or entity affected and the by account type—asset, liability, equity, income, and expense.

Accounts receivable — Money owed to you in the near future by customers for purchases they made from you.

Accounts payable — Money you owe to your vendors in the near future for goods or services you purchased on credit. Accounts payable are usually for goods and services you use directly to generate sales (as opposed to long-term debt, which is debt incurred from buying assets).

Accounting period — The period of time covered by a set of financial statements, usually a month, quarter, or year.

Accrual-basis bookkeeping — A method of bookkeeping that records transactions *when they occur*, whether or not they have been settled by payment.

Amortization – Depreciation of intangible assets, such as "goodwill" or franchise rights that occasionally appear on some balance sheets.

Asset — Something you or your business owns. Assets include tangible things, such as inventory, equipment, vehicles, and buildings. They also include intangible things, such as cash in the bank, money customers owe you, and intellectual property.

Balance sheet — One of three standard financial reports, the balance sheet compares what your business owns (its assets) to what it owes (its liabilities). The difference between assets and liabilities is the net worth of your business.

Bookkeeping — The process of recording the financial transactions of your business.

Breakeven sales — The amount of sales necessary to exactly meet a target gross profit. Breakeven most often refers to the amount of sales required to exactly pay all expenses resulting in zero profit or loss.

Cash (money) — Actual cash or credits that you can use to buy things without going into debt.

Cash (bookkeeping) — A method of keeping books that records transactions only after they have been settled by payment.

Cash flow — The ebb and flow of cash coming into and going out of the business. Profit is but one of the many factors that affect cash flow. In business valuation, the term cash flow is often used to mean EBITDA (see below).

Contribution margin — Another name for gross profit margins. The name reflects the fact that gross profit margins are the amounts left over from sales dollars that are available to pay or "contribute" to paying overhead expenses and profit.

Cost — An expenditure made or a debt incurred in anticipation of a future benefit. If the benefit lasts beyond than the current accounting period, the cost is recorded as an asset. If the benefit is completely used up in the current period, the cost is recorded as an expense.

Debt service — The cash required to cover interest and principal repayment on debt for an accounting period.

Depreciation — An expense that applies to tangible assets such as vehicles, equipment, and buildings. Physical assets wear out and are "used up" over time, which is acknowledged by reducing their values on the balance sheet. In practice, depreciation seldom follows the actual lifetime value of assets but instead is used to "expense" the assets according to IRS rules. Depreciation expense is a noncash charge that allows you to reduce your taxes but distorts the true value of your business.

Double-entry books — Books in which both sides of every transaction— where it originated and where it went—are recorded. Double-entry books include running totals, or balances, for all accounts, not just the bank account.

Draws — Money owners take from the company as a distribution of profit. Draws are not an expense and therefore are recorded on the balance sheet rather than the income statement.

EBITDA – An acronym that stands for Earnings Before Interest, Taxes, Depreciation, and Amortization. EBITDA is most often used to estimate the earning potential of a business independent of who owns it and tax law.

Equity — What your business owes to you, the owner. Equity is what's *left over* after subtracting liabilities from assets on the balance sheet.

Expense — Payments or promises to pay made in the effort to generate sales. (See the definition of cost above.) There are two kinds of expenses:

> *Variable expenses.* Variable expenses go up and down with sales in an accounting period. If sales go up, variable expense goes up. If sales go down, variable expense goes down. Variable expenses include

such things as materials for your product and commissions paid to salespeople. Variable expense is also known as variable cost, direct cost, cost of goods sold, and cost of sales.

Fixed expenses. Fixed expenses do not go up and down with sales in an accounting period. Fixed expenses include such things as rent, utilities, and office salaries that are due each month whether or not you have sales. (They would be due each month for a while, anyway. If you had no sales over a long period, you would adjust your fixed expenses.) Fixed expense is also known as overhead, SG&A (selling, general, and administrative costs), and indirect costs.

Gross profit —What remains after subtracting variable expense from sales. Gross profit is your share of the sales dollar.

Income — Payments or promises of payment flowing into your business as a result of sales. Income is also known as revenue, sales, and sometimes "turnover."

KPIs — Key Performance Indicators are numbers you use to establish a goal (the target KPI) and to track progress toward a goal (the measured KPI). There are an almost infinite number of possible KPIs that can be created from financial statements. One of the hallmarks of great managers is a set of thoughtful KPIs that track and score critical activities that have the greatest positive impact on their businesses.

Liability — Something your business owes to outsiders (nonowners). Liabilities are always intangible obligations and include things such as money you owe to suppliers, your bank, or the IRS.

Margins (percent of sales) — In this book, margins means *gross profit as a percentage of sales*—in other words, gross profit divided by sales.

Matching — The process of recording income and related expenses in the same accounting period.

Net profit — What remains after subtracting fixed expenses from gross profit. (Which is to say, after subtracting *all* expenses from sales.)

Profit and loss statement — One of the three standard financial statements, the profit and loss statement compares sales to expenses. When expenses are subtracted from sales, a positive remainder is a profit, a negative remainder is a loss. The profit and loss statement is also called an income statement or a P&L.

Proper books — Double-entry, accrual-basis books that have been kept current by timely entries and have been arranged correctly. Financial literacy and the ability to make timely decisions depends on your keeping proper books in your business. Well, *not you*, but a bookkeeper or an accountant.

Single-entry books — Books in which only a part of each transaction is recorded, the cash part.

Statement of cash flows — One of the three standard financial statements, the statement of cash flows tells you where your cash went. More than the other financial statements, the statement of cash flows answers the question "They say I make money, so why don't I have any?"

Transaction — An exchange between parties in business—something in exchange for something. Each "something" in a transaction is valued and recorded in books as dollars (or euros, yen, or other currency). There are two sides to every transaction: one side is where the dollars came from, the other side is where they went.

Total breakeven sales — The amount of sales in an accounting period (usually a month) required to *exactly* pay all expenses for that period. It is the point at which profit or loss is exactly zero.

Working capital — The difference between a company's current assets and current liabilities. It is an indication of the company's liquidity; its ability to meet its current cash demands without borrowing. The main elements of working capital are cash, accounts receivable, inventory, and accounts payable.

ACKNOWLEDGMENTS

To the hundreds of small business owners with whom I have worked, thank you. Your courage, dedication and hard work inspire me, and your candor humbles me.

To my parents, John and Helen, you taught me (almost) everything I know.

To my wife, Diane, you are an ideal small business owner, leader, mother, and wife. I love you.

ABOUT THE AUTHOR

MARTIN HOLLAND GREW UP HEARING ABOUT MARGINS AND MARKETS, R&D and sales, and risk and return on investment from his father, a successful entrepreneur. He learned to love the language and rigors of business and grew to believe that business is both the most human of all endeavors and the highest calling. After selling a company in 2011, Martin became a business coach in order to help other owners build profitable businesses that do not require their day-to-day involvement.

Prior to becoming a business coach, Martin operated a group of Nebraska grain elevators and went on to help establish six businesses across a range of industries. His experience has taught him that there are principles common to successful businesses and omissions common to failed businesses.

A native of Norman, Oklahoma, Martin earned a BA degree from Hastings College in Hastings, Nebraska, and a master's degree in business administration from the University of Oklahoma. Over the past nine years, he has worked directly with over 320 (and counting) small business owners to help them reduce stress, reclaim their free time, make better decisions, and earn more money.

Martin spends his free time painting with oils and riding his bicycle. He and Diane, his wife of 42 years, have lived in Norman since 1986, where Diane is the owner of Holland Pediatric Therapy LLC. They have three children and two grandchildren.